STRESS

To Hans Selye's rats who were tortured in vain:
humans are different from rats.

STRESS

THEORY AND PRACTICE

by
Michael King, PhD, M APP SC, M ED, MAPsS
Gordon Stanley, PhD

Department of Psychology
University of Melbourne

Graham Burrows, MD

Department of Psychiatry
University of Melbourne

Grune & Stratton, Inc.
Harcourt Brace Jovanovich, Publishers

Sydney   Orlando   New York   San Diego
London   San Francisco   Tokyo   Toronto

GRUNE & STRATTON AUSTRALIA
30-52 Smidmore Street
Marrickville, N.S.W. 2204

United States Edition published by
GRUNE & STRATTON INC.
Orlando, Florida 32887

United Kingdom Edition published by
GRUNE & STRATTON, INC. (LONDON) LTD.
24/28 Oval Road, London NW1 7DX

Printed in Australia

National Library of Australia Cataloguing-in-Publication Data

King, M. G. (Michael Glenn).
Stress, theory and practice.

Bibliography.
Includes index.
ISBN 0 8089 1874 5.
ISBN 0 8089 1875 3 (pbk).

1. Stress (Psychology). 2. Stress (Physiology). I. Stanley, G. V.
(Gordon Veitch), date. II. Burrows, Graham D. (Graham Dene),
date. III. Title.

155.9

Library of Congress Catalog Card Number: 86–083042

CONTENTS

PREFACE

Stress is understood to be the problem underlying unhappiness and poor health among people. Not surprisingly, stress management is the central tenet in many psychological therapies. Stress is blamed for failures in sporting competitions, and in business management ventures. Stress consultants are paid remarkably well for a few hours of 'common sense'—even when their suggestions have little effect on mood, and no economic effect at all!

As with other areas of science, the unravelling of the mysteries of stress has occasionally made sudden progress. This progress has been followed by periods of consolidation.

Progress is always made by 'giants' of science—people whose names will be remembered. The ideas of these giants are not always 'correct', but they are generally better, or more useful, than the ideas which they replace. There has been little advance in the theories relating to stress and its effects on people for some decades, but there have been many experiments conducted.

There have been plenty of reviews of the prevailing concepts regarding stress and its effects. These ideas have remained unchallenged, perhaps because they were originally the ideas of the scientific giants. There are far too many books which are no more than summaries of the prevailing dogma about stress—even when this dogma is not supported by evidence from experimental work. An example of this is the use of 'relaxation therapy' to treat stress—this method simply does not work! Another example is the efforts made by large corporations to reduce the level of stress in management—the evidence in this book demonstrates that it is neither necessary nor wise to try.

This obvious contradiction appealed to us sufficiently to pool the talents of an internationally recognized psychiatrist (GDB), an outstanding psychologist with the broadest base of research interests (GVS), and a scientifically trained practising clinician (MGK). We felt that we needed to write a book which would take the study of stress, and the practice of stress management, further than others have dared.

Here, we bring together the most recent evidence to challenge some of the standard views of stress, how to control stress, and when to take advantage of it. We have tried to provide a stepping stone which will allow stress theory and practice to advance. Perhaps this book itself takes a new step forward. If we have gone further, it is by standing on the toes of Giants.

ACKNOWLEDGEMENTS

The help of Michael R. Symons, University of Melbourne, is acknowledged, particularly for providing results for various experiments, and for his written contributions to Chapter 2. His criticism of the whole manuscript was also greatly appreciated.

The cooperation of the two Finnish ice hockey teams, ILVES, from Tampere, and LOHI, from Jyväskylä, provided a vital contribution to our understanding of stress and performance at the highest levels of excellence.

Finally, mention must be made of the dedicated goading of Grant Walker and Jeremy Fisher of Grune and Stratton, Australia, who provided the motivation (or was it the stress?) without which this book would not have been written.

The absence of the usual cursory, but inevitably sexist, mention of the 'girl in the office' is not accidental. One of the authors (MGK) typed, edited, and proofread the manuscript, with an inestimable degree of help from his wife Helen.

Chapter 1
INTRODUCTION

The study of stress is not new. There are plenty of books on stress available—many of them by well qualified authors or well known editors. From these books, there is little doubt that stress is of interest to academics. There will always be unanswered questions relating to stress, and so there will always be more books reviewing and musing, but never quite concluding. This volume is not one of them.

Apart from academics, stress is important to clinical psychologists, practising psychiatrists, and medical physicians. Stress is also of interest to police officers, business executives, people at home and at school, army strategists and sporting competitors. These people come to our clinics and ask for help. First, they want to understand how they came to be suffering from stress. Next, they need to know if stress affects their performance, or if it upsets their adversaries (the answer is it does). However, knowing this is not enough. People also want to overcome stress: they can.

There is a need for a book which makes the meaning of stress clear to everyone, one which concentrates upon the present and tells the reader what we know right now about how stress affects humans, one which presents intervention strategies that we can apply right now to change the way that stress disrupts us in the things that we do. The effects of stress upon people, and how they perform under stress have been studied for most of this century, but a readable summary of what we know has not been produced. To satisfy these needs, this book has been written for everyone who believes that his/her performance may be changed by stress, and for everyone who is responsible for reducing (or increasing) the effects of stress on others.

All of us will suffer from stress at one stage or another, some more than others. What we need to know is how stress will affect us, how it will affect our colleagues, and whether we can control it in ourselves. But most important of all we need to know how to cause and manipulate stress in our enemies, in our opponents, and in other competitors in the game of life. In this book, the meaning of stress and the management of stress will be approached in a systematic manner, and the resulting clarity will be of value to academics, to clinicians, and to everybody who has an interest in improving his/her own performance and understanding the behaviour of others.

A. WHAT IS STRESS?

In trying to define and explain human stress, many writers have found it beneficial to use engineering descriptions of forces and their effects. In the engineering sense, 'stress' represents a load applied to a steel beam; when the beam bends the resulting deformation is called 'strain'. For the engineer, then, stress is measured in force or pressure units. Strain is measured in the amount of change or distortion which occurs in the object as it copes with the applied forces.

It is easy to see that in the most general terms human behaviour can be compared to the engineering concept of stress or strain. However, this analogy is only useful up to a point when we are dealing with human behaviour and emotions. It is unfortunate that, in an apparent attempt to give the study of human stress a veneer of scientific respectability, human responses have been linked too closely with the behaviour of steel beams. This has led to a widespread misuse of engineering terms by health professionals.

The principle of borrowing words from other disciplines is of course acceptable, provided that the new use is clarified, and that new definitions are given. However, in order to eliminate ambiguity it is necessary that the new use should remain divorced from the original application. In the case of 'stress' applied to human psychology this separation has not been accomplished and there is still a tendency for writers in psychology to revert to engineering approaches in order to conceive and describe their models of stress.

In this book, the view is taken that stress in humans is unrelated to stress in other systems. Too many predictions about humans under stress have been made from studies which did not use humans, but relied upon studies of laboratory animals. Stress in humans depends upon how we interpret the environment. The general principle that animals and humans take in sensory information, interpret it to some extent, then react to it is true. But this similarity does not mean that animals can be used to show the way humans react to things. Humans process information about the environment in unique ways, so there is only limited value in studying the effects of so-called stress in animals.

The definition of stress being developed here is probably already becoming clear to the reader: stress is a negative emotional experience which results from negative thoughts about our environment. From this, it follows that everyone can experience some level of stress, and this will probably happen each day. This interpretation makes stress sound commonplace and unworthy of further study, but stress is in fact very important. To separate the serious effects from the trivial, the term 'stress' should be reserved for a relatively disruptive level of this negative mood. This position makes the authors critical of popular interpretations of stress which suggest that 'stress is a necessary fact of life' or that 'all demands upon the individual create stress'. These interpretations are in one sense true, but they are as meaningless as the suggestion that obesity is a necessary fact of life, or that all food is fattening. All people eat food, and yet all people are not obese—some are quite the opposite. In a similar way all people face challenges of some type every day, all people can imagine that their efforts might result in failure, but not all people suffer from stress. Before we can begin a sensible discussion about the effects of this mood, stress, we need a more scientific, or more specific, definition of stress.

A scientific definition of stress can be gleaned from the work of Hans Selye (Taché and Selye, 1978), who is often regarded as the most influential person in the study of stress. He investigated the responses to unpleasant or 'noxious' stimuli in animals, mostly rats. He found that a wide range of unpleasant situations (he called them 'stressors') tended to result in a more or less consistent group of physiological responses which he termed the General Adaptation Syndrome (GAS). Another name for the GAS was 'stress'. The results on rats were assumed to apply to humans as well. Selye's work led to a physiological explanation of effects which come from the experience of anxiety. Historically, Selye's work had an important role to play: it showed physicians that serious, long-term exposure to terrible, frightening and unpredictable or uncontrollable events can lead to disease in specific organs.

In experimenting on rats, Selye used electric shocks and other painful stressors. At first glance these stressors seem to be far removed from the stressors in our daily lives. But the physiological link between this work and human stress has been made. Whenever we have serious doubts about coping, then some of the physiological changes described by Selye may occur. That is, negative thinking produces 'stress' in a person. The mere presence of a demand, or a stressor, does not guarantee that an individual will experience stress. On the other hand the absence of an unpleasant and threatening situation does not necessarily mean that the individual will be stress free. Although demands do not always cause stress, it is reasonable to say that as the number or severity of threats and unpleasant demands increases, so the likelihood of a person experiencing stress increases.

While stress depends to some extent upon the direct impact of environmental demands, in humans the stress response is also strongly dependent on the mediating role of each person's interpretation and appraisal of the situation. It is at this stage that the study of stress on humans clearly diverges from the initiating work of Selye (Taché and Selye, 1978) whose study related primarily to animals. The animal studies appeared to support the idea that stress is caused by any stimulus or any demand, whereas the understanding of stress in humans must take account of the highly developed human evaluation procedure. In short, humans think more than rats.

At a later stage in this book we will discuss exactly how to measure stress. These measurements give a more definite meaning to stress, but for the present we should accept that an understanding of stress should include the idea that stress is a state of unacceptable divergence between perceived demands and capabilities to adapt. More briefly, but perhaps just as accurately: *stress arises from doubts about coping.*

B. IS ANXIETY THE SAME AS STRESS?

This question occurs to everyone who studies stress. Doctors refer patients to us asking whether the patient is suffering from anxiety, or only stress. Psychology students always fear that they will be asked to differentiate clearly between the two, and professors shrug off the question with well-practised clichés.

The concept of anxiety has been a central focus of psychology throughout most of this century. Freud saw anxiety as an important component in the development of neuroses. Later writers have discussed the interaction of childhood anxiety provoking events with subsequent personality and achievements. Anxiety is usually understood as an unpleasant state which is evoked by the person's appraisal of the situation. Accepting this description of anxiety, it appears that the answer to our question is more or less 'yes'. But there is room for some uncertainty about the exact equivalence of stress and anxiety. This doubt is mainly due to the extremely wide range of states to which the label 'anxiety' has been applied. Some time ago, for example, in a review of the effects of anxiety upon performance the following terms (from Broadhurst, 1959) were used as interchangeable:

anxiety
ego threat
motivation
activation
arousal
tenseness
fear responses
stimulus
general drive state.

Unfortunately much of the confusion indicated by the above list also applies to 'stress'. The problem has been caused because people who wish to discuss stress (anxiety) have regarded four quite separate parts of the total stress (anxiety) equation as being one and the same thing. The four parts are:

a. An unpleasant or threatening situation, called by experimenters a 'noxious stimulus';
b. A demand to perform, to succeed, or to overcome the threatening situation;
c. The belief that one is unable to succeed; and
d. The consequent emotional response.

Too often, the first three of these separate components are regarded as identical with the fourth, but only this fourth is properly called anxiety or stress. Despite this confusion, the common thread which can be seen throughout the long history of anxiety research makes it clear that anxiety is correctly regarded as the emotional response. By way of contrast, the more recently developed concept of stress was first related to the physiological responses of animals, and only later included the emotional responses of humans. Perhaps, then, if there is a difference between anxiety and stress, it is that the focus of anxiety has been upon psychological aspects of the response, whereas stress has its roots in the physiological studies of Hans Selye. Yet even this distinction is not clear-cut. Freud wrote about the physiological side of the anxiety response; he indicated the important role of heart rate and breathing changes when a baby experiences separation anxiety first at birth. He then suggested that these same consequences of the birth trauma could be seen in adult anxiety responses.

The present situation is that the two words have now converged to be conventionally applied to the same thing, the same emotion. The changing emphasis of fashion has made it more popular to use 'stress'. Perhaps this change reflects nothing more than a desire to use a more 'marketable' term, even though the emotion has not changed. Whatever the reason for the gradual change, the present book will move in step with the current fashion. We will talk about stress, but this does not mean that a distinction between stress and anxiety is implied.

C. AROUSAL AND STRESS

A much more serious issue is raised when we consider the distinction between arousal and stress. Perhaps one of the most common sources of confusion in stress research is the failure to distinguish between arousal and stress. Arousal refers to some aspect of the waking state, and when it is correctly used to describe a mood it applies to feelings of physical or mental activation. There are similarities between the causes of arousal and of stress. Arousal is a non-specific response to a great many different influences. The arousal concept has been mixed up with such diverse phenomena as motivation, reinforcement, sleep, attention, memory, and the effects of novelty (Hennessy and Levine, 1979). Like stress, arousal is affected by the way a person interprets the meaning of environmental conditions. This view of arousal is similar to the ideas of Berlyne (1960). He believed that novelty, uncertainty, conflict and incongruity were factors which caused arousal levels to rise.

Arousal is often understood to be the level of mental 'activation'. This could be taken to mean the person's position along a continuum from sleepy to the other extreme of highly alert. To psychologists who study the processing of information, arousal generally means the quantity of attentional resources which are (or may be) allocated to the current task. Because of the almost overwhelming desire of some psychologists to be taken seriously by physical and medical scientists, it is not surprising to find that the degree of electrical activity in the brain, as measured by electroencephalographic patterns, has been equated with the level of arousal. The alpha waves which tend to dominate the human encephalographic pattern in the waking but relaxed state can be fairly comfortably incorporated into the general picture of what arousal 'really is'. However, telling an athlete about brainwave activity just before a race can never really help him/her to use the effects of emotions in sporting performance.

Arousal is first an emotional state which fluctuates according to demands. The important difference between stress and arousal is that arousal appears to relate to the marshalling of resources to enable one to cope whereas stress is a negative emotion strongly associated with doubts about coping.

D. BOREDOM AND STRESS

Boredom is easily recognised as a condition in which few demands are placed upon the individual, and yet an unpleasant mental state occurs. This unpleasant mental state is quite similar to stress—it probably is stress. If we accept that this unpleasant mood state is an example of stress, then there appears to be a problem of logic. The problem is that stress has been defined as an inability to cope with demands which exceed available resources, while boredom most often arises in low-demand situations:

> Interestingly enough, a low level of demand relative to resources also stresses the body. . . (Colliver and Farnell, 1983, p.33)

> When a person is bombarded with demands which he or she feels unable to meet, a state of anxiety ensues. When the demands for action are fewer, but still more than what the person feels capable of handling, the state of experience is one of worry. . . And finally, a person with great skills and few opportunities for applying them will pass from the state of boredom again into that of anxiety (Czikszentmihalyi, 1975, p. 50).

This apparent contradiction, that low demands produce the same mood as high demands, arises only if we focus our attention upon the person's low level of activity or upon the low demands for output which coincide with boredom. But low demands are not the key to boredom. We are not always bored when there are few demands upon us. The common factors of boredom can include repetitiveness and low arousal, but the additional factors of constraint and unpleasantness are necessary before boredom and stress can arise (Smith, 1981). When these components of boredom—unpleasantness, repetitiveness, low demand task, and constraint—are separated, it is found that constraint plays the greatest role in the development of boredom.

So boredom and stress occur when the person experiences doubts about his or her ability to cope with an excessively unstimulating and constraining environment. Boredom arises when a person perceives a lack of control over the boring situation. Boredom is not due to the level of task demands alone, and although tiredness and lethargy may arise in boring situations, boredom is also not necessarily associated with a low level of arousal. In his review of boredom and its effects Smith (1981) pointed out that both psychological arousal and physical arousal may be either high or low:

> The relation between subjective reports of boredom and physiological changes is certainly not settled. There are reports of both increases and decreases in 'arousal' as subjective boredom increases (Smith, 1981, p. 338).

This interpretation of boredom has the advantage of simplifying the problem of trying to understand the relationship between demand, mood state, and performance. Furthermore, there are some examples taken from real life which appear to support the proposition that the combination of low demands and constraint leads to stress.

Consider the effects of chronic captivity. If it is accepted that, in the short term, constraint and low stimulation lead to stress, then chronic captivity should be expected to lead to chronic stress. Consequences of chronic stress are an expected deterioration of long-term health. This effect on long-term health has been reported (Rahe and Genender, 1983) in studies of prisoners of war. For these captives the uncertainty about the duration of their period of constraint is an additional factor:

> Perhaps the most cruel is the indeterminate length of his captivity. It has been reported that prisoners of war sometimes reflect with envy on civil prisons who have finite prison sentences to serve (Rahe *et al.*, 1983).

Longitudinal studies have shown that overall death rates including accidental deaths were higher in subjects who had been prisoners of war compared with appropriate control subjects and that, following release from captivity, the complete return of both physical and psychological health can take many years. These real-world data confirm the proposition that low stimulation, combined with constraint, leads to elevated levels of stress.

A further example of boredom and stress can be found when the psychological effects of unemployment are examined. Symptoms of stress develop, with the severity of the symptoms being associated with the duration of the jobless period (Fryer and Warr, 1984). When there is a high level of unemployment, the major components of boredom are present. First, a state of 'work deprivation' is generally regarded as being unpleasant; it leads to reduced economic benefits, to lower self-esteem (Breakwell *et al.*, 1984) and to negative mood states (Feather, 1982). Next, being out of work is virtually synonomous with insufficient activity, that is, being confronted with low level demands which are below the person's level of ability. Finally, the important characteristic of constraint is present. People who are unemployed are generally unable to escape from this unpleasant situation. As with prisoners of war, their 'captivity' in the prison of unemployment is for an indefinite period.

In summary, it has been found that boredom is not necessarily caused by low levels of demand. It is only when there is an accompanying degree of constraint and an inability to escape from the unstimulating situation that unpleasant emotional consequences arise. The resulting unpleasant emotion is, in effect, stress. It has the same consequences as stress. Finally, while boredom can arise when there is low arousal, this is neither a necessary nor a sufficient condition for boredom.

E. WHAT DO WE KNOW ABOUT STRESS NOW?

This introductory chapter has alerted the reader to some issues which are central to understanding stress and its effects. We have considered some of the other names that have been applied to stress, and also some of the moods that have been confused with stress. We have established in general terms what stress is and what stress is not. First, stress in humans is a psychological problem which requires psychological understanding. Second, stress is not the same as arousal which is an altogether different state, although both may be altered if a person sees a demand. Third, we have indicated that elevated levels of stress interefere with performance in normal humans.

Let us now consider in some detail the way in which stress disrupts human performance.

Chapter 2
STRESS, AROUSAL AND PERFORMANCE

It is easy to accept the idea that stress along with other psychological mood states can affect performance. The changes that stress can produce are correspondingly well known, and it is quite common to explain Mr Businessman's recent erratic performance as being due to the stress of his marital difficulties, or whatever. The problem with this observation, like other well known facts, is that it doesn't apply in all cases. It is just as common to turn from discussing Mr Businessman's problems and confide to a colleague about the lunch-time game of squash: 'I always do well under a bit of pressure (or stress)'. So what is the truth? Is stress good, or is it bad for your performance? The *general* answer to this question is simple: stress interferes with performance, and the greater the stress the worse the performance. This chapter will discuss some of the evidence which demonstrates this simple relationship. There are some exceptions to the rule that stress degrades performance. This is because there are some exceptional people. These special people are dealt with later, in the final chapter of this book, but the facts that apply to the general population are unmistakably clear: stress is always bad.

At this stage the reader is probably wondering how such a simple proposition can be expanded to fill a whole chapter. In addition, if he/she is familiar with the stress/performance literature, the question will also arise as to how some 80 years of research has never managed to come to a similar uniform, simple and clear conclusion about the effects of stress. Worst of all, the reader may be familiar with a quite different proposition about the effects of stress on performance—the inverted U hypothesis. There is really quite a lot of explaining to do, but to anticipate the explanations a little, this chapter will conclude that: (a) stress is bad for performance; (b) arousal helps to prevent the bad effects of stress; (c) most studies have not considered arousal and stress separately, so most studies are limited in the applicability of their conclusions, or they are simply wrong; and (d) although it has been popular, the inverted U hypothesis is based upon confused theories, incorrect interpretations, and has itself created confusion at the practical level of trying to understand and help people.

Let us begin by reviewing the background to this terrible myth—the inverted U.

A. THE RISE AND FALL OF THE INVERTED U

In its simplest form, the inverted U hypothesis suggests that the best performance occurs when a person is under a medium level of stress. Too little, or too much, stress results in poor performance.

Like many of the incorrect ideas which form the basis of human psychology, the inverted U hypothesis was based upon studies of animals in research laboratories. In 1908, Yerkes and Dodson reported an inverted U relationship between 'drive' and performance for mice. Their inverted U indicated that there was a certain optimum level of drive which caused the best performance, and that at other levels of drive, either higher or lower than the optimum, performance deteriorated. In the Yerkes and Dodson experiments, the performance demanded of the mice was learning to discriminate between the brightness of two pieces of grey paper. Different levels of stress were achieved by giving the mice punishment (different levels of intensity of electric shock) for an incorrect response. On initial appearances, giving shocks to mice according to their selection of pieces of grey paper may appear to be far removed from helping people to understand how stress affects them in their lives. But these experiments and others like them, which used rats and even hens as subjects, have become the foundation of our understanding of human performance under stress.

These ideas have been questioned repeatedly over the years, yet there still remains a general belief that human performance probably displays some sort of inverted U relationship with stress. It is not easy to dismiss the inverted

U hypothesis—it has had sufficient intuitive appeal to remain a force in psychology for nearly 80 years. Broadhurst (1959) listed some examples of published studies which appeared to add credibility to the Yerkes–Dodson Law, as it has become known. The listed examples included an optimum level of air deprivation for speed of underwater swimming in rats. If you were to release rats under water, you would find that they do not swim to the surface as quickly as they would if they had been held under for some time. However, there is an even longer time for which you could hold them under, and this longer period of air deprivation, or drive, would result in a rather slower swimming rate— or even no swimming at all. This and other examples have been quoted as supportive of the inverted U hypothesis. They have also been criticized (Broadhurst, 1959; Naantanen, 1983), but belief in the inverted U hypothesis still lives on.

The inverted U hypothesis was never as simple as the above examples might suggest. From the outset, the inverted U hypothesis included a proposed interaction with task difficulty, with the optimum level of drive being an inverse function of task difficulty. This meant that, as the task became more difficult, so the elusive optimum level of stress was reduced. For easy tasks stress was supposed to help performance; for tasks of intermediate difficulty stress might help performance or it might interfere; for difficult tasks stress was always presumed to be bad. Over the course of 80 years, results of experiments on humans have failed to prove that this complex relationship exists anywhere but in the minds of imaginative academics. But this absence of proof has not dismissed the theory. By appealing to the interaction between task difficulty and the effects of stress on performance, an experimenter can regard the inverted U relationship as compatible with the results of almost any experiment, regardless of the direction of the slope or the absence of a peak in the stress/performance curve. So, although the theory has not been supported by strong and convincing proof, its flexibility has made it difficult to disprove.

For human subjects, supporters of the inverted U hypothesis have generally assumed that 'drive' comes from the desire to do well, and that this is related to social conformity. It has been further assumed that when a person is placed in a situation with any form of threat, however mild, then this drive (desire to appear good, successful and conforming) will result in elevated stress. To this concatenation of psychological jargon, an allowance for individual differences in propensity to become anxious must be added before the inverted U hypothesis can make sense. An 'anxious person' is assumed to evaluate all situations as more threatening than a non-anxious person will, and so for these 'more anxious' people there will be a greater level of stress caused by a particular threatening situation.

It should be noticed how two quite different aspects of a person's appraisal process have been confused in this proposal. The rather weak definition of drive in humans was first linked with the desire to do well. This is reasonable, and it does seem to follow that our performance might improve with an increase in this desire. But quite separate from the desire to do well is the level of stress that people feel when faced with a threat. Under some circumstances, of course, a very strong desire to do well could be the cause of serious worries, doubts about coping, and the emotional response of stress. We only need to remember friends and colleagues who became quite disturbed when they were faced with University examinations: these memories convince us that an overpowering need to do well leads to high stress. But just because we accept that excessive motivation can lead to stress does not mean that all motivation is stressful. Too much exercise is stressful, and sometimes it even kills people in events like marathon runs, but not all levels of physical activity can be regarded as equivalent to stress. Excessive consumption of alcohol can be stressful, particularly the next day, but one glass of beer is not really a stressor. So too, the desire to do well is neither equivalent to, nor a necessary cause of, stress.

It would hardly seem necessary to point out that just because excesses of something are stressful, it does not mean that this 'something' will always be equated with stress. Yet this sleight of hand is exactly what has been going on in experimental psychology for nearly 80 years in order to sustain belief in the inverted U hypothesis. The story, and the supposedly supportive experiments, have not convinced everyone, but the idea has not been totally dismissed either.

This confusion has occurred and continues to occur whenever the definition of stress is not made clear. If a researcher chooses to use the term 'stress' to mean any and all changes in a person's attitudes or emotions (a position supported by Hans Selye, [Taché and Selye, 1978]) then support for the inverted U hypothesis will often be found. In Chapter 4 the definition of stress from a psychological point of view is discussed; for the present discussion, it should be restated that stress is the negative emotional response to doubts about coping. This definition will suffice for the present discussion.

In an early review of the stress/performance literature (Jones 1960, p. 513) it was concluded that the inverted U hypothesis, modified by an interaction with task difficulty 'was altogether too flexible for precise validation. Whereas the great majority of the studies reviewed produced results consistent with that formulation, this consistency was only achieved after a post hoc placement of the experimental situation along the stress–difficulty dimension. The relative difficulty of the experimental task is clearly of importance in determining the nature and direction of group differences... Furthermore it is a factor which can be objectively and quantitatively controlled...but most investigators have failed to exercise this control'.

Jones was critical of the inverted U hypothesis because of the way experiments had been conducted. He pointed out that the inverted U model comes with the built-in excuse that the curve moves about according to task difficulty. As indicated above, the inverted U hypothesis can predict an improvement due to stress, deteriorating performance with stress, or no clear trend at all. It all depends upon where the experimenter chooses to locate his or her optimum 'drive'. To avoid the criticism of 'post hoc interpretation', it is vital that any investigator controls task difficulty, and also measures it. Most investigators have failed to heed Jones' warning. This, however, is only part of the problem.

If studies on stress and performance are to have any real value apart from providing employment for university staff, then there must always be the possibility of finding results the implementation of which can help people. The inverted U hypothesis guarantees that we could never hope to help people to perform better, or to reach their maximum potential. Consider a person faced with a task: an accountant, or for that matter a member of a football team. Under the assumptions of the inverted U hypothesis there will be a certain level of stress which will make our subject perform at his or her best, but that 'best' will depend upon the difficulty of the task. Now for both accountants and for football players, and for most of the people in the world, the demands of the task can change in an instant from being difficult to being easy. The inverted U hypothesis implies that to do our best on a difficult task we need a very low level of stress. On the other hand, for the best performance on an easy task we need a high level of stress. What should a 'motivator' do? Should he or she pre-stress the clients in the hopes that only easy tasks will occur today? Should their stress levels be lowered (assuming that this is possible) in the expectation that all tasks will be difficult? Which will result in the best aggregate performance? This question cannot be answered, so real help cannot be given.

Thus far the main criticism of the inverted U hypothesis has been based upon the serious practical difficulty that it is not a very useful theory upon which to base a practical stress management strategy. Reviews of the literature (e.g., Jones, 1960; Broadhurst, 1959, Naantanen, 1973) have indicated that for a long time there has been scepticism about the possibility of providing sound support from experiments for this very flexible explanation. This might appear to be totally damning for the inverted U hypothesis: there is no practical way to use it. But these criticisms do not in fact make it untrue. We need to find clear experimental evidence either confirming or rejecting the inverted U. Evidence which suggests that the inverted U hypothesis should be discarded is provided in an experiment which is described at the conclusion of this chapter (Experiment 2.1). But before attending to these results we will consider some additional proposals which were also tested in the experiment.

The inverted U hypothesis, although in many ways unsatisfactory, has not been without benefit to psychology. The inverted U hypothesis has served to stimulate a lot of thought and discussion because it has been necessary to explain how such a complicated relationship could occur. Over the years a number of explanations have been invented, considered, and rejected on theoretical grounds and also because they simply could not be experimentally proven. The explanations often blurred the distinction between an undefined motivating force or drive, an externally manipulated stressor, and the actual experienced stress levels. Despite this general weakness, there has been an important thread of continuity in most explanatory theories of the stress–performance relationship. This continuity is provided by the belief that stress alters a person's ability to perceive and to utilize information.

This familiar use of information processing theories has been blended with more recent ways of expressing our understanding of information processing: that the allocation of 'mental resources' is a key issue in human performance (Posner *et al.*, 1980). It has been suggested that these resources are in some way affected by stress (Sanders, 1983). More than this, Sanders developed a theoretical model which included a key role for arousal, both as a mediating variable and as a factor which can affect performance in its own right. This led to a modern restatement of the stress–performance relationship: that stress can affect the quantity of resources available, and with fewer resources a poorer performance will be expected (Sanders, 1983). Sanders' ideas are discussed below and compared with some of the experimental findings which bear upon this proposed relationship.

B. AROUSAL, STRESS AND PERFORMANCE

The idea that resources are involved in the mood–performance relationship has been developed into an arousal–resources–stress–performance model which brings in current ideas about information processing (Sanders, 1983). In Sanders' model, stress arises when there is a perceived deficiency in resources which are needed to cope with environmental demands. This definition of stress is quite orthodox: it accepts that stress is a negative feeling and that it is due to the appraisal process.

Sanders then defined arousal as the availability of mental resources, but at the same time he agreed that arousal can include neurophysiological levels of activation. Arousal is the positive aspect of the human response to a demand. It has been consistently found that arousal is independent of stress; it does not necessarily change because of stress; it is a distinct emotion or mood state (Mackay *et al.*, 1978). Arousal is related to the preparation and mobilization of resources required to cope with demands, and therefore the psychological state of arousal should be expected to coexist with a number of physiological changes. The results of arousal are therefore found in psychological assessment, physiological changes, and behavioural or performance indices. All other things being equal, the more alert and ready for action a person is (that is, the more aroused) the better his or her performance. It would be a tempting, but altogether too simplistic, interpretation to suggest that the speed or vigor of a person's response could be taken as an indication of his or her arousal level. There are too many other factors for this to be a reliable indicator of mood. Yet this technique has been used by self-styled sports psychologists to show 'what sort of person you are', and therefore what sort of help you should seek from them. Beware of these simplistic but appealing interpretations.

After proposing this working definition of stress and arousal, Sanders suggests that their simple effects would be to reduce the level of performance (in the case of increased stress), or to improve performance (increased arousal). However, this description is complicated by the idea that underarousal, which is both the feeling and the fact of having inadequate resources, will under some circumstances lead to increased stress. Underarousal, in this sense, could mean that a person is too tired or fatigued to do the task. In cases where there was feedback to the subject with suggested results, this feeling of underarousal could lead to elevated stress levels. In practical language this means that when people are too tired to do a task they might doubt their capacity to cope and will therefore worry about it and feel bad. But in some cases this increase in stress, corresponding to doubts about being able to cope, might lead to increased 'effort' the effect of which would be to mobilize more resources and thus result in improved performance.

The possibility of this interaction means that it is necessary to measure both stress and arousal in any study of mood and performance. If both moods are not measured, then these interactions interfere with the researcher's efforts to understand the effects of stress. Because of the complex opportunities for feedback that exist between self-appraisal of performance, levels of arousal and stress, and performance, Sanders concluded that performance measures in themselves cannot be considered as any indication of the levels of stress. That is, although stress generally causes poorer performance, under special circumstances a person could be performing quite well, but at the same time be under very high stress.

Although Sanders suggested that 'effort', a concept which was not clearly defined, could lead to better performance, a paradoxical effect of effort is also possible (Simon, 1967). If the degree of effort directed to the task is increased, due to the doubts about coping, this can have a destablizing effect on established 'automatisms' or automatic processes involved in response selection. Performance can then deteriorate dramatically. The disruptive effect of effort under circumstances that increase the importance of 'good' performance has also been described as 'choking' under pressure (Baumeister, 1984). As a real-world example of this structure-breaking function of effort Simon described attempts to improve reading speed:

The initial step in learning to improve one's reading speed is to become aware of the number of stops the eye makes on each line and then to retrain the eye to encompass more content with fewer stops. This is the essence of training in speed reading. However it is a routine occurrence in persons learning to acquire this skill that the initial effect of the effort is to decrease reading speed and reading comprehension... The initial effect of the attention paid to the ordinarily automatic preconscious eye movements in reading has the effect of slowing these movements (Simon, 1967, p. 376).

The effects of stress are now becoming more complex and more difficult to predict. In simple terms high stress may be bad for performance, while elevated levels of arousal should be an advantage. Furthermore low arousal can lead to poor performance in the first instance, and then it can lead to a subsequent increase in stress. But this last combination may be altered by increased effort which raises arousal and improves performance. On the other hand, this increased effort might paradoxically interfere with performance by disrupting the automatic allocation of mental resources.

All of these proposals incorporate the idea that mental resources and the allocation of attention is important. There is also a clear suggestion that arousal cannot be ignored in studies of stress and performance. Finally, the alternative paths leading from the effects of increased effort provide a hint of an issue that will be developed later in this book: the existence of different, but stable or enduring, stress–performance effects in different types of people. For the moment we will review the results of some experiments which provide support for this somewhat confusing theoretical picture.

C. UNDERAROUSAL AND PERFORMANCE

First, there is the proposition that underarousal might lead to poorer performance. Being in a state of underarousal means being sleepy or tired. The evidence which enables the low arousal state to be regarded as the same as being sleepy is discussed in Chapter 4.

The effects of underarousal upon performance appear to be fairly easy to investigate: this can be done simply by depriving people of sleep, and then giving them tasks to do. The problem with this approach is that, within reasonable limits, simply asking people to stay awake does not guarantee that they will be 'dearoused' or sleepy during the critical experimental period: they may make more effort for the experimenter. This difficulty has been noted (Kjellberg, 1977). It has masked the expected effects of sleep deprivation on performance in many experiments. Perhaps the most elaborate experiment in the sleep deprivation domain involved a group of combat soldiers who were kept on a three hour per day sleep regime for up to nine days. Their performance was monitored in target shooting, navigation-type exercises, and a variety of other tasks which were relevant to military performance. Only minimal effects on the experimental tasks were noted (Haslam *et al.*, 1977); however, major examples of non-compliance with experimental demands and other gross behavioural irregularities were noted, *in the periods between the formal tests of the experiment.* Sleep deprivation certainly had serious performance effects, but these could be voluntarily overcome during specific periods of testing.

The history of sleep deprivation studies has been summarized by Kjellberg (1977), and he concluded that:

a. When performance effects have been noted, they are consistent with the view that sleep deprivation leads to dearousal;
b. That the performance changes due to the dearoused state were in the negative direction, that is, underarousal leads to worse performance;
c. *But* that effects on performance were often rather small, apparently because the person noticed the inadequacy of his or her own intrinsically dearoused state which accompanies the experimental condition of sleep deprivation. Upon noticing the state of dearousal, the sleep-deprived person apparently makes more effort, thus achieving a satisfactory performance. Performance decrements were therefore most noticeable in situations where there were low obvious performance demands, and little performance feedback; and
d. The way in which performance was degraded under dearousal conditions was not so much an overall deterioration, but rather a more uneven performance with intermittent periods of unresponsiveness—periods which were called 'lapses' (Williams *et al.*, 1959).

These findings are in line with some of Sanders' (1983) predictions. It seems that dearousal potentiates a negative effect: poorer performance might occur under low arousal. The work on low arousal has pointed out the *direction* of the effects, as well as indicating the *way* in which arousal affects performance: low arousal leads to lapses.

Low arousal can also lead to increased 'effort' which would ultimately produce a performance which is not any different from 'normal'. Now Sanders (1983) suggested that, in conditions which stemmed from the state of under-arousal, elevated levels of stress were involved in the feedback loop which causes the regrouping and elevation of resources. Therefore we find that in the interpretation of arousal effects, we are continually led back to the effects of stress.

D. THE EFFECTS OF STRESS

Sanders (1983) proposed that stress is bad for performance, and that this effect can be predicted from a resources model. But what Sanders' model did not explain is what happens to the resources that seem to go missing under the effects of stress. Logically, these resources may somehow be 'lost' altogether, which would mean that there would be a consistently reduced level of ability under stress. An alternative explanation is that the allocation of the resources may be intermittently disrupted from time to time. Notice that this second explanation is quite similar to the established effects of low arousal. The two explanations have appeared in one form or another over many years, although they have not been deliberately contrasted, and critical experiments to select between them have not been conducted. If we are going to understand the effects of stress on human performance, and allow for these effects in real life situations, then we really need to know just how stress interferes with the use of resources.

Unfortunately many experimenters have been content to observe a change in overall performance, but the investigators have not noted *how* this change occurred. An example of an experiment which included a proposal about the mechanism of the stress effect involved the effects of cold water immersion on mental functioning. In this experiment, men were submerged for three hours, clad in diving suits, in water of 4.5°C. Mean core temperature dropped by 0.5°C during the three hour experimental period. Performance was measured by tasks which included the detection of targets in the peripheral visual region, and solving navigation exercises. The three hour cold exposure, reported as resulting in 'stress' by the experimenter, had a deleterious effect on the tasks. It was concluded that the manifestations of stress were due to the: 'extreme and unusual environmental conditions [which] compete with task-relevant simuli for the attention of the observer, and interfere with his (*sic.*) capacity to respond to the task requirements' (Vaughan, 1977, p. 104).

Baddeley (1972) also reviewed evidence relating to the deterioration of performance under anxiety provoking situations in simulated deep sea diving. When subjects believed that there were potential dangers in a pressure chamber, they showed a 'clear anxiety response in terms of . . . subjective ratings' and 'they also showed a clear decrement in detection of peripheral light signals but no drop in performance on the central task' (Baddeley, 1972, p. 453). Baddeley suggested that, in an effort to cope with the stress invoked by the supposedly dangerous environment, the stressed person experiences a narrowing of focus of attention to one aspect of the situation or task, and: 'if this aspect happens to be the task he (*sic.*) is required to perform, then his efficiency will be increased. If not, however, his performance will deteriorate . . .' (Baddeley, 1972, p. 543). Notice that Baddeley worded this explanation to cover the possibility of either an inverted U effect, or just reduced performance. However, his review of these environmental stressors did not include clear evidence of an inverted U hypothesis—only a deterioration in performance, or no change. In the absence of any sign of improved performance, Baddeley's (1972) explanation about the narrowing of attention effectively means much the same as Vaughan's (1977) proposal: cold water immersion can result in a reduction of available attentional resources, and peripheral visual tasks demonstrate the effect first.

The failure to detect peripheral targets, interpreted as a narrowing of the visual field, may seem unrelated to the availability of attentional resources, but in fact the two are linked. Peripheral vision can be suppressed as a response to the limitations of the observer's ability to cope with the quantity of information available (Mackworth, 1986). So, if there is a reduced amount of attentional resources available, this is expected to correspond to a reduced processing efficiency with respect to information in the peripheral regions of the visual domain (Taylor, 1982).

Baddeley's (1972) review and Vaughan's (1977) experiment were typical of so many of the studies on stress and performance. They noted certain changes in performance, they linked these changes to the allocation of attention, but they did not critically test for the underlying mechanism that they inferred from these changes. Their explanations of the mechanism were coloured by the prevailing belief in an inverted U function, and by a commitment to the notion of narrowing of attention. They did indicate that at moderate (or somewhat severe) levels of stress, performance changes for the worse. But did the experiments really let us know anything important or new about stress and performance?

The first cause for concern in interpreting these experiments is that the effect of arousal was ignored in both studies. This is unfortunate, since exposure to cold has a real, demonstrated, and undisputed effect on both physiological and psychological arousal. One effect of cold exposure is an increase in metabolic rate. This increase in metabolic rate produces more heat, thus combating the excessive heat loss. A simultaneous effect is the restriction of blood flow in peripheral blood vessels to reduce body surface temperature. Both of these changes are effected by alterations in circulating hormones—many of these hormones are associated with elevated levels of stress. But does that mean that the normal body responses to cold can be interpreted as stress? The cold induced thermogenesis effect can provide up to 180% of normal resting heat production, but does the increased metabolic rate mean that the psychological mood state of arousal is also increased? Finally, if core temperature does drop, a state of mental lethargy and incompetence follows. This state is perhaps similar to the condition found in severe sleep deprivation situations, it is recognizable as a state of dearousal, but generally is not accompanied by any of the signs of stress. Indeed people in advanced hypothermia often seem quite care-free.

In the studies presented here, it is reasonable to accept that stress was indeed elevated in the subjects. For example, Baddeley pointed out that participants in a simulated dive experiment should have the potential dangers emphasized in order to cause anxiety. However, it remains unfortunate that the expected changes in arousal were ignored.

Putting aside this question regarding the possible intrusive effects of changes in arousal, it is possible that the results could help our understanding of the mechanism underlying the effects of stress upon performance. A distracting effect was noted, but it was not indicated whether this distracting effect was continuous or intermittent. It was simply reported that some type of distraction of attention had occurred, and that this was demonstrated by an overall reduction in the detection of peripheral targets. It was not possible to say exactly how this distraction manifested itself.

It is possible that the distraction effect of stress is quite similar to the effect of dearousal: that is, an intermittent effect. A stress-induced, intermittent disruption of our attention to the task in hand is easy to equate with what we have all experienced when trying to work under stress. Patients suffering from stress come to our consulting rooms with the complaint that they cannot concentrate; students stare vacantly at their books during examination time while their minds are elsewhere, or just nowhere. Everyone has experienced this inability to concentrate due to stress. There is also reference in the literature to the idea that competing stress-related stimuli interfere with the subject's ability to concentrate on the task in hand. But intuitive appeal and common sense interpretations do not guarantee that an explanation is correct. Experimental evidence supporting this possibility must be found.

Reports of experiments have been published which can be used to test the idea that the same mechanism underlies both stress and arousal effects, if stress-induced changes in performance have been compared with dearousal performance deficits. When similarities have been found, they can be taken to suggest that both stress and arousal manipulate attention allocation in the same manner. This could mean that the effect of stress is intermittent.

Evidence supporting the idea of a shared mechanism has been forthcoming. For example, a similar reduction in overall performance was obtained either by producing 'cognitive fatigue' as an after-effect of a high attentional demanding task, or by exposure to a stressful situation (Cohen and Spacapan, 1978). In this case the demanding (tiring) task was a laboratory experiment involving a computerized reaction-time task. The stressful situation was achieved by having the subjects complete a demanding series of checks of prices of items in particular stores. For example in a bookstore, the task was to find out the 10 best selling books, and to check their prices. Under the supposedly stressful condition, the subjects had to deal with eight different stores within a period of 30 minutes. The experiment was carried out in a crowded shopping mall. Unlike many of the so-called stress experiments which have been criticized, in this instance the experimenters administered a questionnaire which assessed the degree to which the subject found the environment to be crowded and unpleasant. The degrees of perceived mental effort and physical fatigue were also measured. Finally, after either the tiring task or the stressful situation, the subjects were assessed on their approach to an apparently real life helping situation. Both tired and stressed subjects were scored 'low' on this helping task. The subtlety of the final performance task enabled the experimenters to eliminate some of the problems of subjects making a greater effort. The results here cannot demonstrate the intermittent disruption to attention allocation, but they do point towards the similarity of the effects of high stress or low arousal.

The compounded effects of high levels of anxiety together with high memory load were also found to impair performance on logical problem solving tasks (Gross and Mastenbrook, 1980). The depletion of attentional resources, which is essentially the same as 'cognitive fatigue', has also been suggested as the mechanism involved in stress-related deficits on problem solving tasks by other investigators (Heuser, 1978; Deffenbacher, 1978).

E. DISCUSSION OF EXPERIMENTS

The experiments discussed above seem to add empirical support for the proposition that the effects of elevated stress are similar to those of dearousal, but, although the effect of stress on performance has been studied for nearly 80 years, there have been few attempts made to clarify the mechanism of this effect, and fewer (if any) which have simultaneously attended to the effects of both stress and arousal. Given these problems, some experiments conducted by the authors are described in order to simplify and clarify the effects of stress and arousal.

The experiments are appended to this chapter. The first, Experiment 2.1, employed a visual task to study the effects of stress and arousal on target detection. The experiment was designed to satisfy all of the criticisms that Jones (1960) had made of the typical stress–performance studies. That is, stress was measured using a validated scale, and item difficulty was also measured. A full range of task difficulty was present, ranging from items which everyone succeeded on (difficulty approaching 0) to items in which almost nobody detected the target (difficulty approaching 1). The mood levels on both scales ranged from very high to very low. In short, the experimental conditions covered the complete range of variation on the factors which have been supposed to interfere with the confident demonstration of an inverted U function.

The second experiment, Experiment 2.2, pushed the study of stress and arousal into the real world. A team of soccer players was studied over a series of matches. The stress and arousal levels of each player were recorded during the games, and these mood scores were compared with each player's performance.

In summary the results of these studies indicated:

a. That only linear effects of stress and arousal upon performance were present—there was no evidence of an inverted U relationship nor of any other curved function;

b. That the way both stress and arousal affect performance is through the modulation of intermittent breaks in attention, or lapses;

c. That the effects of stress and arousal are found in laboratory tasks and in real sporting performance; and

d. That an interactional interpretation of stress and arousal provides the best explanation of the effects of these two moods upon performance.

1. Discussion of results

a. The inverted U relationship

The clarity of these results appears to conflict with the enduring notion that there is an optimum level of stress which comes from an inverted U relationship between mood and performance. Although only linear trends with either of the mood states were found, the study reported here is not inconsistent with the possibility that apparent inverted U relationships could occur in some experimental situations. The identification of arousal as an important mood state which responds to environmental and task demands and which has an effect opposite to that of stress has provided a possible mechanism for creating an inverted U relationship between externally defined 'drive' and performance. The confounding of the two orthogonal mood states could produce an inverted U pattern of results between 'mood' and performance.

For example it was shown (King et al., 1983) that the demand associated with a 10 minute administration of the Ravens Progressive Matrices served to elevate arousal levels, but left stress levels unchanged. The results of the experiments reported here show that increased arousal improves performance. Therefore if externally defined 'drive' were to be experimentally manipulated by two conditions (no pre-test, Ravens pre-test) then the results would show an increase in performance due to 'drive'. If a third condition were devised consisting of a difficult pre-test which proved ambiguous, tiring, frustrating and confusing to the subject, such a test might be expected to elevate stress (e.g., Cohen and Spacapan, 1978). This would lead to reduced performance. These three points, no pre-test, Ravens test, and the frustrating pre-test could be wrongly interpreted as representing a hierarchy of increasing experimentally induced drive. The results would then be reported as another demonstration of the inverted U curve, provided that the experimenter did not measure either stress or arousal, but simply relied on intuition to equate 'drive' with stress.

Another way of obtaining the inverted U curve is to use physiological change as a definition of stress. The difficulties of equating stress to physiology are discussed in the following chapter, but the inescapable experimental results cannot be ignored. As above, first consider very high stress with its consequential poor performance. Virtually every physiological function is changed by very high stress levels: blood chemistry, urine content, heart rate and its correlates, skin resistance, and so on. Whichever index is used, the subject will be in a state that we can call 'physiologically high' under this extreme stress condition. The second point on the curve, again as agreed above, will be 'physiologically lower' and the assessment of performance will show normal results—that means better than under high stress. The third point is logically defined by a situation where the person is 'physiologically low'. During sleep, or near sleep, virtually all physiological markers are in this 'low' state; during sleep or near sleep virtually all tasks are performed worse than under normal conditions. So the third point must indicate an inverted U curve. Naturally the experimenter may not have selected such extreme points as the folly of this would be too obvious. Nevertheless any properly conducted experiment which ignores arousal, does not measure mood state, and defines 'stress' in terms of physiology, must produce an inverted U curve. The foolishness of this approach cannot be overstated, and the artifactual results cannot be accepted.

It is now clear how some laboratory experiments could misleadingly appear to support the inverted U hypothesis. With complete acceptance of misleading interpretations, self-styled stress consultants suggest that a little bit of stress is normal, or that it is just as bad to be understressed as overstressed. 'When demands and available resources match each other, we have an optimum stress level. . . a low level of demand relative to resources also stresses the body. . .' (Colliver and Farnell, 1983).

In summary, the results above support the idea that the two separate mood states stress and arousal have opposite effects upon performance. Stress has a simple deleterious effect while arousal enhances performance. If we confound these two moods, measure neither, and ignore task difficulty, then we just might come up with an apparent result of an inverted U relationship between something and performance. The inverted U interpretation has served only to prevent useful predictions being made in this domain. Finally, the inverted U theory has allowed at least one generation of 'stress consultants' to make extravagant claims which could not be easily refuted at the time, but which could never help people to improve their performances.

b. The incidence of lapses

Our experiment with the soccer players showed convincingly the effect of stress in real life. Stress causes poorer performance, but its effects can be modified by increased arousal. The results of the laboratory experiment first enabled us to reject the inverted U hypothesis, and second provided a means for analysis which showed the mechanism of the stress effect: this effect was due to response 'blocking' or 'lapses'. The results of both the laboratory study and the field study were quite similar in the directions of the trends they showed. In particular, the laboratory work showed why stress and arousal can interact in practice: they both have an effect upon the occurrence of lapses. The arousal results represent an important step in the clarification of our understanding of the effect of this mood upon performance. The results do not support the idea drawn from Sanders' theory that arousal directly affects the availability of resources in a relatively stable way. Instead of this, an intermittent effect was found.

The proposition of a fluctuating effect of mood upon performance is not at all new: the novelty here is that the effect has not been previously linked to both stress and arousal in the one experiment. It is a pity that after nearly 80 years of research on this question it was necessary to conduct yet one more experiment to clarify the action of stress and arousal. The need was there, but now that the critical experiment has been presented, its results can be seen to stand in line with a whole host of comparable, but never quite conclusive, findings.

Distraction has often been alluded to as a possible source of error, (for example Deffenbacher, 1978; Hockey and Hamilton, 1983) or cognitive failures (Broadbent et al., 1982). The distraction effect of low arousal was first described in the phenomenon of response blocking (Bills, 1931, 1935; Teichner, 1971). These 'mental blocks' which affect performance more during periods of low arousal were later termed 'lapses' (Wilkinson 1963, 1969; Williams et al., 1959; Broadbent, 1953). The findings which support the distraction hypothesis also indicate that normal processing takes place between lapses: 'The performance between these [blocks] should, according to the hypothesis, be more or less unaffected' (Kjellberg, 1977, p. 145). Bergstrom (1972) studied sleep loss (arousal?) together with the threat of an electric shock (stress?) upon performance, but he measured neither stress nor arousal and so his conclusions were necessarily weak.

In the laboratory, response blocking has generally been investigated in the context of vigilance or serial processing tasks in which continuous input is received by the participant and a continuous response is required. But more realistic tasks have also been occasionally studied. It is evident that in an exercise where a rapid response is required—in competitive sports like football, for example—lapses in attention could regularly coincide with moments when a critical decision is needed. During a lapse the player will probably miss the ball, but at other times the play will be unaffected. The overall effect will be fewer possessions, as we found in the present studies. Another report described a different task in which lapses can lead to noticeable failure—flying in a helicopter (Stave, 1979). In this case the pace of the task is to some extent controlled by the pilot and therefore the coincidence of a lapse with a critical moment is expected only rarely. In a long (simulated) flight with several key tasks required at specific times, it was observed that lapses did occasionally coincide with a critical moment. The result was a serious mistake which affected the success of the 'mission'. Although the results of laboratory experiments show that lapses occur at the rate of more than one per minute, in this simulated flight scenario the coincidence of a lapse with a critical decision period occurred only about once every two hours.

Taken together, the theories, the literature, and the present results point to the fact that lapses in attention are the key to the stress–performance relationship. The relationship between 'blocks' and either stress or arousal was never made clear, but it has always been possible that they were somehow linked. Now we know that lapses are in the order of a few seconds duration, and that the problem of lapses increases with higher levels of stress. We also know that increasing arousal can restore performance to normal. Having established these effects, an important and practical next step in the study of stress is to describe practical methods that are used to measure it.

2. Experiment 2.1

a. Analysis 1: Linear or curved effects of mood on performance?
A laboratory experimental task was devised to show the effects of stress on performance. The results were first analysed to determine the presence of any hint of a U-shaped relationship.

(i) Background to experiment
Studies of the effects of stress have frequently used a visual task to measure performance. This is not surprising since visual tasks are relatively easy to control in the psychological laboratory. Also visual tasks appear to be relevant to the real world situation, where we are strongly dependent upon our sense of sight. There are good theoretical reasons for studying the visual system too. Although the process of 'seeing' is consciously perceived as an immediate process, the truth is that a high degree of processing is necessary to make sense of our surroundings (Shiffrin and Schneider, 1977; Treisman and Gelade, 1980). We can more or less instantly recognize the presence of well learned, highly familiar objects, but for most tasks we need to successively sift through the information, sorting and classifying and grouping it. This means that a high proportion of our attentional resources must be directed to the task of seeing, otherwise errors may occur.

Now, for a task which places a high load on available resources, the distraction (or lapse) hypothesis would predict that more errors would occur under higher levels of stress. This means that when a person is under stress, then errors may be expected on visual tasks. This would be particularly so when a fast response is required, even though a more accurate decision might be available at a later time.

Examples confirming the occurrence of visual errors under stress are available from real world cases. In military combat situations, a fast response is required, and the people involved would reasonably be regarded as being under stress. In this situation, inadequate processing of visual information, coupled with the perceived demand for action, might lead to a chain of automatic responses being triggered by an inadequately processed set of visual data (Shiffrin and Schneider, 1977). In simple terms, the brain is understood to say 'shoot first and ask questions later'. Inappropriate action may follow the incorrect identification of objects as targets. A military colleague related a story from Vietnam when his platoon opened fire on a monkey in a tree. The occasion was their second night in Vietnam—a clear case of the 'shoot first...' principle being applied in unfamiliar and stressful circumstances.

Other examples of inappropriate actions during combat have been reported. In World War I, clashes between allies who had been in combat for a long time occurred (Schmidtke, 1976). In the Pacific arena during World War II, Australian planes were attacked and shot down by their American allies, apparently because the red in the Australian markings (roundels with red centres, then white and blue) were mistaken for the Japanese markings which also featured red (a red rising sun). For the psychologist, this represented a fascinating example of an identification task which required the viewer to integrate information about two visual dimensions: colour and shape. Under the stress of combat conditions, the identification was based upon a single feature only: the presence of red. This led to 'false positive' sightings. For the Australians, this represented a quite unwanted additional hazard. The incidence of these false positive sightings by United States fighter pilots had become such that by the end of 1943 it was decided to eliminate red from the Australian markings altogether (Pentland, 1980).

Closer investigation under safer circumstances has confirmed the general proposition of visual processing errors under stress. For example, in an experiment using a digit recognition task, the incidence of false positive results increased for subjects under the stress experienced before a first parachute jump (Simonov, 1977).

In summary, there is a solid body of evidence from experiments and observations to suggest that errors due to stress should be noticed on a visual search/detection task. Notwithstanding earlier comments that the results of laboratory experiments do not necessarily reflect the situation in real life, it was decided to devise a carefully controlled visual task, but one which used 'real world' stimuli.

The task used a set of 80 stimulus slides selected from a large number of slides that had been taken for the purpose of comparing different military uniforms in various outdoor environments. These stimuli were found to be particularly useful since the participants, both civilian and military, could perceive the real world relevance in the task. The selected group of slides was chosen to provide a wide range of difficulty with targets in the foreground, some targets concealed among bushes, and others containing no targets at all.

This task satisfied Jones' (1960) first criticism that task difficulty is either unknown or uncontrolled in many stress experiments.

The characteristics of this particular task have been described in detail (King et al., 1984). The important points for the present analysis are:

a. That there was a range of difficulty from 0 to 1;
b. The reaction time to detect a target was closely related to task difficulty and was not affected by the speed/accuracy trade-off which usually affects only simple (low processing demands) choice reaction tasks; and
c. If the target was not detected then the NO TARGET response took the total time available (three seconds) regardless of the 'normative' difficulty level.

Subjects were asked to search for the presence of a target, a man in uniform, among the bushes. For each participant the number of YES responses, that is, the number of detections, was summed over the 80 slides and this value was used as an index of that observer's performance (SCORE). The mood state of the subject was assessed using the Stress/Arousal Adjective Check List measure of stress and arousal (King et al., 1983).

To test for the presence of a curved function relating either stress or arousal with performance the square of the mood state was computed. Thus, for example, if an inverted U function of performance with stress (ST) were found, then the data would fit a parabolic equation of the type

$$\text{SCORE} = a\,\text{ST}^2 + b\,\text{ST} + c \tag{1}$$

would be expected, where a, b, and c are weighting constants. To support the notion of an inverted U function a negative value for the coefficient a would be required.

In the case of a significant coefficient for the quadratic coefficient a, the optimum value of stress could be computed from the point of inflexion of the equation:

$$\text{ST(optimum)} = -b/2a \tag{2}$$

A similar equation would apply for the arousal variable, AR, if it were related to performance with an inverted U function.

The measure of performance was the total number of targets detected. The results showed significant linear effects were due to both mood states stress and arousal. The analysis showed no support for the notion of an inverted U function between performance and stress: neither the stress nor the arousal quadratic coefficient was significant. For stress there was evidence of a steady straight-line reduction in performance as stress increased. Similarly in the case of arousal, the curve was linear over the range of AR scores, that is from 0 to 10. As expected from Sanders' (1983) model, the results indicate that performance can be increased in a linear fashion with increasing arousal. The linearity of these effects was indicated by the individual correlation coefficients: performance with stress, correlation = -0.30, significance = 0.004; performance with arousal, correlation = 0.19, significance = 0.012. These significant effects were in the expected directions, but they are relatively low. The main reason for the modest size of the simple correlations based upon performance–mood across a number of people is that individual differences in ability are confounded with the effects of mood. The significance of the correlations indicates that the effects are real, but the importance of these effects is not reflected by the magnitude of the correlation coefficients.

b. Analysis 2: Removing individual ability from mood effects

To eliminate the effects of individual differences in the effects of mood on performance, a further correlation analysis was conducted.

For each item, the average stress score for the subjects who responded YES was calculated (STY), and the average stress score for those who responded NO (STN) was also calculated. Similarly for arousal, the average arousal scores for those who responded YES (ARY) and for those who responded NO (ARN) were calculated for each item.

The effect of mood state on performance which has already been demonstrated above could be shown again, providing that these STY and STN values were meaningful. These effects were in fact found: the correlation of STN with item difficulty being -0.75 $(P < 0.01)$ and with ARN the value was 0.70 $(P < 0.01)$. The significant negative relationship for stress indicates that while all subjects would be expected to respond NO to high load items, only highly stressed subjects would respond NO to relatively easy items. Thus a higher STN value would be expected for low load items. Taken across all items, a negative slope would be expected. The interpretation for the AR result is again supportive of the notion that elevated arousal is a facilitator of performance.

This analysis is more complex than the first, but its consequences are simple. The results are in the same direction as those from Analysis 2, but the stronger correlations provide grounds for greater confidence in the proposed effects. Because this expression deals with average values, the effects of individual differences in ability are not included in the variance. Taken together, the high correlations of STN and ARN show that, after individual differences in ability are removed, a great deal of the variation in performance can be explained in terms of stress and arousal effects.

c. Analysis 3: The lapse hypothesis

The distraction hypothesis suggests that there is an intermittent interruption to the progress of normal data processing when lapses occur due to stress. This distraction means that on a prolonged task such as that described above, even for relatively easy items a highly stressed subject might on some occasions not detect the target and would therefore respond NO. On the occasions when distraction did not interfere with normal processing, the stressed subject would complete items in a manner which would be indistinguishable from the performance of an unstressed subject. This 'normal processing' would occur where the subject responded YES.

It is assumed that the incidence of lapses is not affected by the task itself: lapses are not stimulated by specific levels of item difficulty. Thus there should be no relationship between item difficulty and average stress level of the subjects who responded YES to each item. Similarly for arousal, there should be no relationship between task difficulty and average arousal level of the people who were able to detect the target.

It has always been suggested that high stress, and low arousal, lead to poor performance—and the results from the first two analyses confirm that this was the case in the present experiment. The role of an intermittent distraction, particularly in the case of stress effects, has not been clearly predicted. If lapses did not occur, then another possible explanation for the overall reduction in performance, indicated by a reduced number of targets detected, would be that there is a consistent and continuous attenuation of the availability of cognitive resources. That is, a person suffers from a reduction in 'ability' while under the effect of stress. This reduction in ability due to elevated stress levels would mean that only the least stressed people would detect the target on the most difficult items. To put it another way, the average stress level of those who responded YES to difficult items would be necessarily low. For the easiest items, it would be different. Even allowing for a reduced level of ability due to stress, virtually all people (those with high stress levels and those with low stress levels) would be expected to detect these easy items. Thus the average stress level of those who respond YES to the easy items would be similar to the average stress level of all subjects.

Taking these two extremes together, the suggestion that poor performance under stress is due to an enduring attenuation in ability would demand a 'normal' stress value, on average, for those who detect the easy items, but a low stress value for those who detect the most difficult items. This is the same as saying that there will be a significant negative correlation between task difficulty and average stress level of subjects who detect the target.

To summarize the expectations, the intermittent lapse hypothesis suggests that targets will be missed regardless of their difficulty; however, if the effect of stress is to produce a constant reduction in ability, then there will be an association between item difficulty and stress for those detecting the target.

With regard to arousal, Sanders (1983) proposed that this mood state is intimately linked with available resources, with increasing arousal being associated with improved performance. Other work which studied low levels of arousal related to performance under sleep deprivation. The most consistent interpretation of sleep-loss effects has been that it causes an intermittent breakdown in a person's ability to concentrate (Kjellberg, 1977). These breaks have been studied as 'blocks' (Bills, 1931), or 'lapses' (Williams et al., 1959). The arousal data can be analysed in a manner analogous to the stress data, and a comparison of the two should provide a clear answer as to whether or not stress causes lapses.

To test for the possibility that lapses were responsible for both stress and arousal effects in the present performance task, further analyses of the data were conducted.

(i) Results

Testing for the mechanism of the mood state effect upon number of target detections, the product moment correlation coefficients between item difficulty and the two values STY and ARY were calculated. These correlations were -0.04 (STY), -0.07 (ARY), neither of which were significant. The lack of a significant correlation for YES responses supports the lapse hypothesis as the mechanism of distraction for both stress and arousal.

At this stage we should restate the question and reconfirm what the answer means. The lapse explanation means that there are intermittent, more or less total, interruptions or lapses in a person's allocation of attentional resources. From time to time they see and process nothing. The assumed random nature of this process would mean that no relationship would exist between target characteristics (difficulty, for example) and the mood of those who saw the target.

The results showed the absence of the required correlation. This supports the intermittent distraction hypothesis for both stress and arousal. It is always difficult, however, to claim that one has proven a point by the *absence* of an effect. The unpleasant alternative explanation is always that the results are themselves random. The correlation of 'rubbish' is generally zero, and therefore the present results could indeed mean just nothing. This possible objection must be taken seriously. The item difficulty data has been shown previously to be robust and meaningful (King et al., 1984); this left the new way of expressing the mood data (STY and STN) as the 'rubbish' candidate. However, these two computed variables had already been shown to be particularly valid representations of the average performance of the subjects. The validity of these values was demonstrated by the high correlations with performance (above 0.7) in the earlier analysis. Therefore, it is reasonable to accept that the mood effects found in the present experiment were due to intermittent interference with the allocation of attentional resources. Furthermore, this interference had no relationship with the specific demands of each item, that is, item difficulty.

(ii) How long is lapse?

The analysis above established the importance of lapses in explaining the effects of stress on performance. A final question which arises relates to the duration of a lapse. The same results were used to answer this question.

It had been found that, during a lapse, people missed the target, and therefore responded NO at the end of the three second exposure time. The task was automatically timed at one new item each three seconds. The chance of a YES or a NO response from a particular observer for any individual item can be calculated using a Rasch analysis procedure. In brief, this compares the ability level of the observer with the difficulty level of the task (Wright and Stone, 1979). When the observer responded NO to an item which was easy, relative to his or her normal ability level, this was signalled as an 'error' by the Rasch analysis procedure. The number of errors in a string could therefore be used to estimate the length of a lapse.

There are some uncertainties involved in this procedure, as the task was not specifically designed to enable the computation of lapse length, but at least a general idea of lapse duration could be obtained. The result was that average lapse length was 2.0 items long (that is, about six seconds), while the typical maximum was 3.3 items, corresponding to ten seconds. The task lasted for four minutes, and there were on average five lapses in that period. The effect of stress was to increase the duration of lapses.

Previous work with lapses in the literature used self-paced tasks. With self-paced tasks, a new item is not presented until the person gives a 'ready' signal. The slowness to respond to a single task item was the means by which a lapse was detected, but the duration of a lapse had not been demonstrated, but the notion of a lapse lasting a matter of a just a few seconds is compatible with the general theory. Future work is necessary to establish lapse characteristics more clearly. In the meantime the present analysis is sufficient to confirm that lapses do occur, they last longer under the effects of stress, and that they are probably of sufficient duration to interfere with many real life tasks.

3. Experiment 2.2

a. Sporting performance and stress

Sporting performance is of special relevance to the study of stress and performance. With the input of large sums of money into sports at all levels, there has naturally been a considerable interest in obtaining the best performance from the sporting participants. Many sporting competitions appear to take on the appearance of major military campaigns, and this increases the chance of the participants becoming stressed. Sport is now a serious business, and the lessons of stress and sporting performance under stress apply to other serious areas of life as well.

The interaction between stress and change in arousal predicted by Sanders (1983) is expected in situations where the players know how well or how badly things are going. In a soccer match, the players do have knowledge of results. They know if the team is winning or losing, and on an individual basis they also know whether or not they are getting possession of the ball. With the Sanders model in mind, the present study was designed to test the idea that stress reduces performance in 'real life' circumstances, but that changes in arousal might interfere with the stress effect.

The players used were a university first graded team of football (soccer) players. Stress and arousal were measured using the LASS (Linear Arousal and Stress Scale). The LASS is a rapid measure of stress and arousal devised specially for use in sporting competitions (King and Symons, 1985). It is described in more detail in Chapter 4.

Players completed the LASS whilst on the field warming up immediately before the game, at half time, and also at the conclusion of play.

Each player's performance was assessed by totalling the number of possessions during each of the two halves of play. This procedure was repeated over six successive games during which a core of 13 players were used. The median number of games for each player was five.

(i) Results

Statistics relating to mood state and performance scores are presented in Table 2.1, where P1 and P2 represent possessions for first and second halves respectively.

The simple effects of mood upon performance are demonstrated by the Pearson product moment correlation coefficient between possessions and mood state. These correlations were computed for each of the two halves. Table 2.2 presents these figures. The negative correlations show that increased stress reduced player effectiveness. Arousal had little direct effect although the one significant result was in the direction to indicate that increased arousal has a beneficial effect on play.

A further analysis of the figures was designed to show any interaction between stress and arousal. The figures in Table 2.2 indicated that mood states after the game (ST3 and AR3) were not related to performance. This was not surprising since a different set of thoughts, feelings, and demands are involved in the formation of post-game moods. The present analysis was concerned with relevant changes in mood, and therefore only the first half game statistics were used. For this analysis ST represented mean stress over the first half (that is, the average of ST1 and ST2). Similarly AR is used as the mean of AR1 and AR2.

To test for the interaction effect, a backwards stepwise regression analysis was performed on all players' statistics. This 'backwards stepwise analysis'

Table 2.1. Means and standard deviations of mood state scores and performance statistics ($n=69$).

	Mean	Standard deviation
ST1	3.2	2.3
ST2	3.5	2.2
ST3	3.1	2.2
AR1	7.0	2.0
AR2	6.5	2.5
AR3	5.8	2.2
P1	16.2	5.7
P2	15.8	4.5

P1 = first half possessions
P2 = second half possessions
ST1 = stress before game
ST2 = stress at half time
ST3 = stress after the game
AR1, AR2, AR3 = arousal before, mid-term, and after the game.

Table 2.2. Correlations between mood scores and performance

| | correlations with performance: | | | | | |
	ST1	ST2	ST3	AR1	AR2	AR3
P1	−21	−27	n	n	n	n
P2	n	−38	n	n	22	n

(All correlation coefficients are multiplied by 100; only those significant at $P<0.05$ are shown).

simply means that first all the mood variables (ST, AR and the interaction ST*AR) were grouped together and tested for a combined effect on performance, then those mood variables which made no contribution to the effect on performance were removed. The remaining significant variables were ST and ST*AR. The elimination of AR as an effective variable indicates that arousal (AR) alone had no direct effect on performance. The mathematical expression linking mood and performance was:

$$\text{PERF} = a - b*\text{ST} + c*\text{ST}*\text{AR}$$

where a, b, and c are positive constants.

The value of the constants in the equation would depend upon specific outcomes of each game, such as average number of kicks. For example, for this soccer players experiment, the value of *a* was 19 kicks. The importance of the equation is obtained, not by a specific consideration of the numerical value of the constants, but by looking at the *direction* of their effects.

If stress was very low for example, that is approximately zero, then players' performance would be expected to tend towards the value of the constant *a*, since both of the other terms in the equation would be multiplied by the near-zero value of stress. Elevated levels of stress would tend to reduce the expected number of possessions, since the second term in the equation has a negative constant $(-b)$.

However if the elevated level of stress was accompanied by high arousal, then the positive c*ST*AR term would be in the directon to cancel out the negative effects of stress. High arousal could therefore counteract the negative effects of stress upon performance.

The results from this real-life study are in accord with the predictions based upon Sanders' (1983) resources model. Sanders predicted that increasing stress would reduce performance while the influence of arousal would be to counteract the normally bad effect of elevated levels of stress.

Chapter 3
IS STRESS PHYSIOLOGICAL?

Whether or not stress is physiological is an important concern. In this chapter, we intend our discussion for people who are interested in psychology, and especially interested in a fuller understanding of how an emotional state like stress can affect the entire organism that reprsents the human being; that is, the mind and body. The discussion is also relevant for those who have been led to believe that the way humans think and feel can be understood through instrumental measurements of what the body is doing. They will be shown that this second-hand method of trying to understand human thinking and feelings is inappropriate.

We have found that all sorts of demands can cause changes in the body chemistry (generally referred to as the physiology) of animals. It is also true that these changes are likely to occur in humans when they experience stress. The results of animal studies have been important in that they provided a clue as to how the body behaves under stress. However, it is not wise to take the results of animal studies and apply them directly as if they tell the whole story about people. The way we humans interpret our environment plays an important part in the development of stress. Whether or not this same appraisal process occurs in animals, it certainly plays a central role in the development of stress in humans.

If we return to an examination of reactions and put aside the appraisal process for a moment, we can demonstrate that a number of physiological changes occur when a person experiences stress. If we want to study the total effects of stress upon performance, then it is necessary to have an understanding of all the effects of stress upon both mind and body. As well, we should have an appreciation of the other reactive mood state, arousal. Only when we have understood the changes that stress produces can we decide upon the best way of measuring stress. It has already been indicated that there is some ambiguity in the psychological understandings of what stress is, or is not. Perhaps because of this uncertainty, there has been a tendency for people who are investigating the effects of stress to define stress as a physiological phenomenon, with the psychological issues being regarded as of only secondary importance. A physiological phenomenon should of course be measured through physiological methods. Whilst this encourages the employment of physiologists, these physiological measures are seductively attractive to the investigative psychologist. Physiological measures have the great advantage that they are not subject to bias due to the attitudes of the subects being studied; social desirability does not influence the data collected. The tendency of some people to always answer 'yes' (or always 'no') to questions (that is, response set) is not a problem. Furthermore, these physiological measurements add the concrete irrefutability of the physical sciences to an investigation. The only problems arise when the investigator attempts to ascribe psychological meaning to these results.

The present chapter will review some of the physiological changes that often accompany stress. We will see that these changes are not universally associated with stress alone; therefore, they cannot be regarded as fundamental definitions of stress. We will also see that there are often interactions between physiological changes and the psychological mood state of a person. These interactions mean that it is not possible to say that one change or one emotion causes another change. All the effects of stress on our total mind-body system are interconnected. There are many feedback loops where the excesses of one response are counteracted by another response. The overall picture is a combination of the efforts of the mind-body to retain—or return to—a state of equilibrium within itself. At the same time the organism, the person, tries to deal with the effects of external demands and attempts to reach equilibrium with the outside environment, in the process having to face external threats, demands, and problems.

A. CAN STRESS BE DEFINED PHYSIOLOGICALLY?

The investigations of Hans Selye (Taché and Selye, 1978) and others led to the proposal that long-term exposure to many different noxious agents always tended to bring about three morphological changes. These changes were: (i) hypertrophy of the adrenal cortices; (ii) atrophy of the thymus; and (iii) gastric ulceration. Typically this work was done on animals. The experimental animals had no power to alter the aggravating or harmful circumstances. They were in effect tortured slowly until they became very sick. The animals were finally killed and their internal organs examined for damage. This work indicated that the above triad of effects always occurred and that the effect was non-specific. This non-specific response was called the stress response. Of the three proposed 'non-specific stress responses', attention has been mainly directed towards the adrenocortical system in studies with humans, perhaps because short-term activity of this system can be used as a relatively convenient measure of acute reactions to the environment.

Table 3.1 shows the average effect of a demand, usually regarded as a stressor, on each of a number of biochemical markers. The method of sampling is also indicated. The method is itself an important aspect of the measurement procedure, since where a blood sample is required the procedure can be stressful for many people.

Earlier investigations generally relied upon monitoring epinephrine (otherwise known as adrenaline), norepinephrine, or cortisol levels. Circulating levels of these substances do tend to change in response to any demand, and this finding supports the somewhat circular argument that when stress is defined by these changes then stress is found to be the response of the body to any demand. In line with improved analytical tehniques there is now a wide range of endocrine changes which correspond to humans being in a situation of either anticipated or experienced stress (Rose, 1980).

Unfortunately, the increasing sophistication of biochemical analysis has not been matched by parallel advances in our understanding of how these changes are related to human moods. In the earlier stages of the physiological study of stress, it was proposed that stress was a non-specific physiological response. Therefore it was common to monitor just a small number of biochemical markers in order to indicate the onset of stress. However, as analytical techniques improved in their sensitivity, specific differences in the endocrine responses have been associated with particular stressors. These findings led Mason (1968) to question the proposed universal nature of the stress response. In fact, with careful analyses it seemed to be true that each different 'stressor' produced a different profile of responses in the body chemistry system. In summarizing this situation, Cox (1978), p.67 stated that: 'the more stimuli studied, the more distinctive the eliciting profile for each component

Table 3.1. Some suggested physiological stress markers, method of sampling, and their direction of change

Marker	Sample	Change under a demand
cortisol	blood	raised
17-hydroxy-corticosteriods	blood or urine	raised
catecholamines		
epinephrine	urine	raised
norepinephrine	urine	raised
fatty acids	blood	raised
growth hormone	blood	raised
glucose	blood	raised
prolactin	blood	raised
testosterone	blood	depressed
cholesterol	blood	raised
uric acid	blood	raised

of the physiological response becomes. . . the integrative mechanisms controlling the response appear to be organized to react selectively in producing patterns of multi-physiological change which differ according to the specific stimulus'.

So we have the situation that the profile of the 'non-specific' response to a demand has been steadily and reliably shown to be determined by the demand, and by other factors too. Differences have been observed in the pattern of endocrine responses associated with different so-called stressors. For example, during exercise the levels of epinephrine and norepinephrine are both elevated, whilst emotional stress tends to raise epinephrine levels in particular; some hormonal levels are apparently elevated only by severe stressors. Compared with the period of exposure the period of elevation differs from one marker to another (Rose, 1980).

Selye and his colleagues (Taché and Selye, 1978) did not accept the suggestion that their non-specific physiological stress response was in doubt. The stressor-specific responses could be explained by the fact that different stressors can interact with specific biochemical stress markers and inhibit the proposed non-specific response. It is for this reason that they claim it is necessary to employ a battery of tests to indicate the presence of stress by physiological methods (Taché and Selye, 1978). Far from clarifying the situation, however, the use of a battery of measures has only served to underline the impossibility of defining stress in terms of human physiology.

Differences in the pattern of biochemical changes over time were shown in a study of men experiencing apprehension regarding jumping from a parachute training tower (Ursin et al., 1978). This study, employed a battery of measures to study the coping process. The general effects were in the expected direction. After repeated exposure to the jump tower there was an overall reduction in the physiological reactivity of the men. That is, they were beginning to show the development of the coping process. But not all of the biochemical indices showed the same return to normal levels as the coping process continued. For example, norepinephrine and growth hormone remained somewhat elevated while self-reports of stress, and some other hormonal measures, indicated that no further stress was being experienced. It remained unclear from that study why some of the commonly used biochemical markers continued to be elevated prior to successive jumps from the tower, even though self-reported stress, and some other chemical indices, indicated that coping had occurred. This difficulty in interpretation emphasizes an important point of the development of stress; either the anticipation or the experience of environmental events may have an effect upon the body chemistry, but these changes do not always correspond to the normal understanding of stress. Studies such as this one provide physiological evidence for the existence of more than one reactive state; the additional concept of 'arousal' should also be recognized as a physiological and psychological fact. Arousal is just as important as stress, it is associated with some of the same physiological changes as stress, but it is quite independent of stress.

Regardless of where we start our study of stress, we are inevitably led to the idea that the process of perception and interpretation of demands is part of the key to the understanding of the human stress response. Again, this has been shown in a study of men training for a leadership role (Rahe *et al.*, 1982). The course was designed to be intensive and demanding. The results of the chemical analyses showed that cholesterol levels were elevated in those subjects who reported that they found the course to be stressful, while uric acid levels were elevated in subjects who did not appear to have doubts about coping. Notice that if Rahe *et al.* (1982) had neglected self-report data, their report would have been quite different. They would have been able to say:

a. The course was designed to be intensive, and it was indeed stressful because some of the candidates dropped out;
b. Both cholesterol and uric acid levels were, on average, elevated due to the demands of the course; and
c. Therefore the experience of stress can be measured by either uric acid or cholesterol changes.

Reports claiming to understand psychological consequences through the collection and analysis of blood or urine have been regularly published. They will probably continue to be published. It is a pity that the apparent validity of biochemical analyses is so attractive to editors of learned journals. It is a refreshing sign that groups like those of Rahe (1982), or of Ursin (Ursin, 1978;

Vaernes, Ursin *et al.*, 1982) are beginning to incorporate psychological measurements in their investigations.

So far, we have seen that the modern study of stress developed out of studies on animals, studies which seemed to show a universal bodychemistry reaction to unpleasant conditions, or in fact to any 'demand'. At first it seemed possible to apply the same story to humans, but two problems arose. First, the so-called stress response depended upon the nature of the stressor. Second, depending upon the way a person was thinking and interpreting things, the response may have included changes which indicated stress, or arousal (that is, the sense of preparedness to meet the challenge). Since stress and arousal are independent, and certainly not mutually exclusive, the changes in physiology could also indicate the elevation of both stress and arousal levels.

In summary, there is now sufficient evidence to indicate that changes in body chemistry (in levels of adrenaline, for example) do not always mean that a person is stressed. It is possible to conduct carefully controlled laboratory experiments where the only change is a shift in stress levels. Under such circumstances a corresponding physiological change may run exactly parallel to stress. It is also possible to torment captive animals until they show a certain set of physiological signs. Neither of these situations relates to real world experiences, and therefore the results can add little if anything to our understanding of how stress develops and how it affects our performance.

B. INTERACTION OF MOOD STATE AND BODY CHEMISTRY

Under stressful conditions various physiological changes occur. These changes depend upon the way a person is thinking, and upon the person's mood. An important feature of these altered levels of circulating hormones is that the changes can themselves have an effect upon mood state. Some of the hormonal changes tend to exacerbate the effects of negative thoughts, while some of the changes have the effect of reducing stress levels. A balanced treatment of the physiological dimension of stress must take account of the effect these changes have on mood state. The combination of these interactions between mood and body chemistry is that some of the physiological changes which are observed under the influence of a stressor may not indicate that stress is being experienced: rather they might indicate that psychological equilibrium is being maintained due to the release of mood stabilizing chemicals.

This interactive relationship between body chemistry and mood state will be discussed below. First, however, we will draw attention to and then sidestep a contentious 'red herring'. A logical corollary of the proposition that changes in body chemistry can cause changes in mood state is the idea that at least some instances of chronic stress may be due to metabolic disease. That is, in theory at least, there may be a number of forms of endogenous anxiety that are due to abnormalities in brain neurotransmitter and receptor function, autonomic nervous system regulation, or basic metabolism.

This notion that there may be an underlying biochemical cause for stress is appealing to those who are involved with the development and use of drugs as a therapy for stress-related problems. If a biochemical abnormality is not just associated with, but is actually causing stress, then the use of chemotherapy can be viewed as an attempt to treat the actual cause rather than the effects of stress. On the other hand, there are those who try to understand how people çan become stressed, and try to help them to deal with their problems. This latter group may prefer to believe that at least in the majority of cases the biochemical irregularities associated with stress are the result, and not the cause of the mood state disorder. Longitudinal studies which seek to distinguish between these two propositions are rare, although one careful study which included provocative endocrine tests on patients one year after their last mood disorder concluded that the biochemical abnormalities were the result and not the cause of the patients' problems (Kathol *et al.*, 1984).

No single study can be expected to settle this issue of causality. The complexity of the issue itself is confounded by the forces of multimillion dollar industries and professional interests. The discussion which follows will not try to deal with the issue of causality. We will discuss some of the biochemical changes which are usually related to stress, and show the way these changes interact with the way a person feels. This discussion will indicate that levels of stress may be elevated, maintained, or reduced by the action of some of the biochemical changes that occur when a person notices or anticipates a threatening situation.

Any proposed treatment of the biochemical side of stress is necessarily difficult in a psychologically oriented book. There are many complete volumes written on the endocrine system alone, and to attempt to cover the physiological system from a mainly psychological viewpoint must lead to a compression of important issues, and to potentially misleading overgeneralizations. However, to provide a background for the discussion of the biochemical aspects included later in this chapter, a basic description of some of the functions of the human energy system follows.

Human energy is based around the production and use of glucose. Carbohydrates that occur in human food are broken down and stored in the liver as glycogen. Between meals, glycogen is broken down and glucose is released into the blood in order to keep blood glucose at a relatively constant level. Most of the glucose in the blood is removed and used by cells, including the brain and the muscles, to provide energy. The breakdown of glucose by cells can be divided into two stages: anaerobic, in which no oxygen is required, and aerobic, in which oxygen is essential. In the first of these processes, the by-product is lactic acid. A number of hormones have an effect on this glucose control procedure, and therefore they affect the availability of energy resources. This in turn alters the person's feeling of strength or weakness. These same hormones are involved in the stress response.

1. Epinephrine (adrenaline) and norepinephrine (noradrenaline)

Epinephrine, or adrenaline, is perhaps the most widely known of the hormones which change when we notice a demand. For the purposes of this review, norepinephrine may be regarded as similar to epinephrine. Their actions are in many ways similar, but the major sites from which the hormones are released differ.

In the event of an apparent emergency, circulating levels of epinephrine can rise quickly. Epinephrine elevates heart rate and tends to cause sweating. It stimulates the liver to break down glycogen to glucose quickly and therefore provides a potential source of energy. Because of this action, the elevation in adrenaline level is often interpreted as an adaptive preparatory response. It is easy to find psychological writings which make this sort of claim. It is even possible to appeal to a clouded view of evolution and point out that the extra production of glucose would aid our ancestors in confronting the threat of an advancing, hungry sabre-toothed tiger. Those who did not produce the extra energy-giving glucose, so the story goes, were eaten and so they did not have the opportunity to pass on their faulty, low glucose-producing genes.

But there is a problem with this simple story: it is not based upon observable facts. Most life-and-death competitions with real life opponents, whether they be modern street fights or imagined contests with prehistoric carnivores, are concluded quite rapidly. An initial and immediate surge of strength is usually the deciding factor. We already have enough energy stored in our muscles for the first decisive few moments of a life-and-death struggle. All of that circulating extra glucose will never be needed to protect our genetic endowment. And there is a further problem with the 'preparedness response' story. The real effect of epinephrine is that it *reduces* the rate at which muscle cells remove glucose from the blood. Thus, elevated levels of epinephrine may be associated not only with the mood of stress, but also with the feeling and the fact of being weak. Stress does not necessarily result in a biochemical response which will lead to enhanced performance. In its most normal form, the stress response could be associated with impaired or weaker performance.

This weakening effect of stress and the interference with activity has been reviewed and refined into a story which is compatible with observable behaviour, and also with the observable biochemical dimension of stress. Gray (1981) has shown that by considering the action of antianxiety drugs it is possible to indicate the main site in the brain which is the seat of anxiety, and it is also possible to better understand the effects of anxiety itself. Gray pointed out that it has become common to regard the benzodiazepines as the only effective antianxiety drugs. This belief is fostered by the observation that there are sites in the human brain which specifically bind the benzodiazepines. The easy conclusion is that we now know almost all there is to know about anxiety and its treatment. That conclusion is easy for those who would prefer to regard stress (or anxiety) as a biological disorder which requires biological treatment. But Gray (1981) has pointed out that, historically, other drugs have been found to have antianxiety properties as well. The barbiturates were used in this role in the prebenzodiazepine era, and alcohol is still used by many sufferers of stress. These two alternative drugs are quite effective, but they are not presently the preferred treatment. The preference of the medical profession for the benzodiazepines is not based upon the ineffectiveness of the older treatments, but upon the fact that there are fewer unwanted side-effects associated with the newer class of drugs.

Taking note of the effects of the three types of anxiety drugs, we can arrive at an alternative core of evidence about the effects of stress. Combining his observations of behaviour with neurological evidence about the effects of these drugs, Gray (1981) concluded that the suppression of activity was one of the inevitable signs of stress. He even coined a specific name for a system in the brain which causes this suppressing effect—the Behavioural Inhibition System (BIS). He outlined the neurological evidence for the existence of a stress-activated inhibition system in the brain, and suggested that when stress arises 'there is an immediate inhibition of any motor program...(and)...an interruption in the function of higher-level systems concerned with the planning and overall execution of motor programs' (Gray, 1981, p. 195).

The relevance of Gray's work to be epinephrine effects is that both predict a reduction of behaviour, or behavioural effectiveness, under conditions of stress. Gray did not anticipate that a suppression of activity would occur at the muscular level—he believed that the Behavioural Inhibition System was a single factor located at a single site in the brain; the septohippocampal region. He scarcely considered the effect at the local level of muscles, and specifically proposed that the inhibition was at the planning level, not the output level, in the brain: 'it is not supposed that this (inhibition) function is exercised directly at the point of motor output' (Gray, 1981, p. 196). When Gray's evidence of suppression of planning processes and reduced output of motor signals is combined with the physiological evidence of reduced potential energy stores at the muscle level, then the reported negative effects of stress are strongly supported.

In addition to controlling blood sugar levels, epinephrine is thought to have a direct effect on our thoughts and feelings. The psychological effects of epinephrine were studied by Schachter and Singer (1962). People injected with epinephrine were exposed to different social atmospheres in which companions acted either euphorically or angrily. The emotion reported by the subjects depended upon the social context. Subjects exposed to a euphoric companion reported euphoric feelings, whereas an angry companion stimulated angry feelings. The interpretation of this report was that elevated epinephrine levels may intensify any emotion that the person believes is appropriate. Unfortunately, the findings of this experiment have never been replicated (Cotton, 1981). In a recent review of all the evidence it was concluded that there was no convincing evidence for Schachter's (1962) claim that epinephrine is necessary for an emotional state, nor for the suggestion that emotional states may result from a labelling of unexplained 'arousal' due to the effects of epinephrine (Reisenzein, 1983). This absence of proof has not prevented sports psychologists from taking money for their treatment of 'misinterpreted arousal'. We are aware of practitioners who suggest that the problem of 'before race' nerves can be understood as an example of the effects of epinephrine being misinterpreted by the athlete, leading to inappropriate emotions. Naturally a 'treatment', based upon a rejected theory can do little good for the athlete.

2. Growth hormone

This hormone is essential in the regulation of the normal growth of a child. Apart from its action in stimulating growth, growth hormone is also important in the regulation of blood sugar. It is secreted by the anterior pituitary gland and its effects with respect to blood glucose are essentially opposite to those of insulin. It stops most of the cells in the body, in particular, those of muscle, from taking glucose from the blood. However, it has no effect on the uptake of glucose by the cells in the brain. Typically the output of growth hormone is increased when the blood glucose levels fall and decreased when the blood glucose rises. For example, just after a meal when the blood glucose concentration tends to be high, insulin levels are also high and growth hormone output is low. This balance stimulates the cells to use glucose. When the meal has been absorbed and blood glucose falls, the level of growth hormone increases, making a barrier to the entry of glucose into the cells. The regulation of growth hormone is complex, being responsive to a number of different physiological stimuli including blood glucose levels, the effects of various amino acids, and also to different stages of sleep. In addition to responding to the demands of physiological homeostasis, growth hormone is also responsive to psychological stimuli.

The elevation of serum levels of growth hormone is generally found during the elevation of stress. In many ways, growth hormone tends to correspond to other stress-related endocrine responses, with elevations being reported after surgery, physical exercise, watching stressful movies, stressful interviews, written and oral examinations, venepuncture, and the administration of psychological tests (Rose, 1980). Elevated growth hormone is found in anticipation of a stressful event, and the anticipation elevation can be even larger than the increase caused by the stressful event itself (Rose, 1980).

The growth hormone response, although found on average in a group of people under stress, is not found universally in all those who demonsrate other endocrine stress responses (elevation in the levels of catecholamines, for example). This finding has led to the proposition that the growth hormone response is mediated by some personality characteristics of the individual under stress. The studies of growth hormone changes are beginning to be understood as evidence of a biological correlate of coping style, rather than as a marker of the presence or absence of stress. Specifically, defensiveness or neuroticism appears to be associated with growth hormone responsiveness. Relatively low levels of anxiety were needed to provoke a growth hormone response for people with higher levels of defensiveness or denial, that is, the 'emotional' styles of coping (Kosten et al., 1984).

In summary, like other biochemical indicators of stress growth hormone is commonly raised by a wide variety of stressors, but in some individuals the growth hormone response does not occur. Further investigations of coping style have shown that the growth hormone response is marked for people who are rigidly defensive and who use emotional styles of coping with problems, such as denial. The non-responders are people who may still experience elevated stress as measured by psychological assessment or endocrine changes, but who do not usually resort to defensiveness or denial to deal with problems.

3. Endorphins

It has become very popular to blame almost any mood-related effect on endorphins. There are several reasons for this, but not one provides a serious scientific basis for the extravagant claims made about endorphins. For the serious psychophysiologist, endorphins are best regarded as an excellent answer for a question that has not yet been asked. The appeal in explaining psychological responses in terms of endorphin effects lies perhaps in the fact that they are a relatively recently discovered class of compounds. Their effects, and the exact mechanism of these effects, are at present poorly understood. They are mysteriously related to the opiate class of drugs, and because of this relationship, almost any claims about their effects seem to be accepted or at least tolerated.

During the 1970s, receptors were found in the central nervous system which interacted with opiate-like compounds. This suggested that some normally occurring substance existed which could bind to these opiate receptors.

The substances discovered were shown to have properties similar to those of morphine, and they are generally referred to as 'endorphins', that is, endogenously occurring morphine-like substances. Further study has demonstrated different groups of compounds with similar activities, but it is proposed that for the present discussion the term endorphin should be used to cover all these endogenous polypeptides.

It has been suggested that elevated endorphin levels are involved in a number of psychiatric disorders including the experience of anxiety (Atkinson *et al.*, 1983). The endorphin involvement is that, first, endorphins are released in association with elevated levels of anxiety. Second, it is expected from studies with the opiates that the action of these endorphins would be to calm the patient and to counter the anxious mood state. The findings of current, and in some instances tentative, research indicate that a dependence upon endorphins may be involved in some cases of chronic anxiety disorders. At first this seems to be paradoxical since endorphins are believed to make people more calm. The suggested mechanism is that, as a consequence of stress, people often resort to habits or to some form of ritualistic activity as a coping mechanism, and that either the anxiety or the habits are somehow associated with endorphin release. Thus, habit disorders can be interpreted as part of a process which relieves the experience of unpleasant emotions including stress.

The effect of morphine, and probably that of the endorphins, is inhibited by the opiate antagonist naloxone. Based on this effect, naloxone has been used in a number of imaginative studies which tried to establish the presence of an endorphin effect. If elevation of the levels of endorphins occurs too frequently, it is suggested that a dependence upon endorphins could occur. This dependence would involve a consequent rise in the frequency of the need to display the habit disorder. Examples of these habit disorders include constant checking of doors, locks, position of furniture, the straightness of paintings on the wall, and checking for the cleanliness of one's underwear. Persistent eating, leading as it does to obesity, is also classed as a habit disorder.

Some studies appear to support this connection between endorphins and habit disorders, but too often the studies have been on animals. In experiments on rats, a number of studies have looked for a link between anxiety caused by tail pinching, subsequent overeating by the rats, and apparent dependence upon endorphins as indicated by naloxone effects (Antelman and Rowland, 1981; Morley and Levine, 1980). This 'tail pinching' means that the animal is subjected to continual pain by having its tail pinched. Tail pinching is believed to make the animal anxious—and it probably does. It is further believed, or hoped, that rats with a pain in the tail somehow represent anxious humans. Some results of these experiments on animals were encouraging and led to the speculation that an addiction to endorphins was involved in the maintenance of overeating habits in obese humans. If there were such an association between endorphin activity and overeating, and of course obesity, then the endorphin antagonist naloxone would be expected to produce opiate withdrawal symptoms in obese humans. These symptoms include changes to heart rate, skin temperature, skin resistance, respiration rate, and pupil size. This proposition was tested on a group of obese people (O'Brien *et al.*, 1982). No withdrawal response occurred with the administration of naloxone. This experiment was interpreted as providing no support for the existence of a relationship between elevated levels of endorphin activity and human obesity. This finding demonstrates that one should proceed with caution when speculating on the role of endorphins in human behaviour disorders. The results also underline the point that, to extend our understanding of human psychological functioning, we should rely primarily upon studies of humans. If we give rats a pain in the tail, we do not necessarily advance our understanding of people with problems.

More supportive of the endorphin addiction model was a case report which involved patients with obsessive-compulsive disorders (Insel and Pickar, 1983). After naloxone was administered to the patients they became acutely absorbed in their self-doubts and checking habits. This acute exacerbation of the symptoms continued for up to 24 hours. The study seemed to show that there was a dependence upon endorphins and that this dependence was associated with the behaviour disorder. The growing understanding of the effects of endorphins in these patients with obsessive-compulsive behaviour disorder has not as yet led to a proposal for treatment.

Exercise has been found to be useful in the treatment of people who suffer from anxiety. Some of the theories which seek to explain why physical exercise should relieve stress include an endorphin-based model. There is an elusive feeling of well being, sometimes known as the 'jogger's high' which comes with prolonged exercise. It is commonly suggested that this could be due to the release of endorphins in the brain (Stein and Belluzzi, 1978). This idea has immediate appeal since it is understood that endorphins can serve to modulate pain and to improve mood state. Those observers of the jogging phenomenon who do not actually participate in the activity cannot understand how people can claim to enjoy an activity which causes aching muscles, blistered feet, blackened toenails, and respiratory distress. For these observers, a drug-induced state of false euphoria is an attractive explanation. This explanation has received some support from studies on animals. For example, studies on chronically exercised mice showed that the animals developed a dependence on endorphins. From this it was suggested that: 'it is tempting to speculate that this finding may provide an explanation for anecdotally reported behaviour changes in marathon runners and others who engage in a regular, daily exercise regimen. If deprived of their daily exercise such people claim to suffer a withdrawal syndrome characterized by anxiety and irritability' (Christie and Chesher, 1982, p. 1176).

Yet once again the mice were tormented in vain. The involvement of the role of endorphins in exercise-mediated changes in mood state has been rejected by direct experiments with people (Markoff *et al.*, 1982). When naloxone was administered to humans, the beneficial mood-elevating effects due to running were unaltered. It now appears that mood changes caused by running are not due to the effects of endorphins.

In summary the levels of endorphins have been found to be elevated by anxiety. Their effect is to reduce the severity of a negative mood state, or to induce a feeling of well-being and euphoria. The beneficial stress-reducing effects of exercise are probably not associated with endorphins. There are conflicting views on the role of endorphins in the maintainance of stress-related overeating and obesity. There is some evidence that chronic anxiety patients may have become addicted to the presence of elevated endorphin levels, and that their continued anxiety attacks and other behavioural disorders may be associated with this addiction.

4. Lactate

The idea that exercise helps 'everyone and everything' is very popular, particularly among runners. Whether or not endorphins are involved, exercise is still regarded as a good thing to do if you are anxious. It is ironic, therefore, that an important area of anxiety research is concerned with the intolerance of exercise by anxiety patients. This work related to the role of lactate in the physiological understanding of stress.

In the 1950s, it was noted that patients with anxiety neurosis produced excessive amounts of lactate with standard exercise. Their characteristic anxiety symptoms were also precipitated by exercise and occurred at a time of rapid rise of blood levels of lactic acid (Jones and Mellersh, 1946, Cohen and White, 1950; Linko 1950; Holmgren and Strom, 1959). Patients who exhibited 'effort intolerance' and who developed anxiety symptoms when exercising had lower oxygen consumption during vigorous exercise compared with normal people. A shift to an anaerobic metabolism and increased muscle oxygen debt was thought to account for the elevation of levels of serum lactate with exercise.

Pitts and McClure (1967) hypothesized that lactate itself could produce anxiety attacks in susceptible individuals. They conducted a double-blind study of the effects of sodium lactate infusion on patients with anxiety neurosis. Fourteen patients and 10 control subjects were injected with either sodium lactate, sodium lactate plus calcium chloride, or glucose in sodium chloride. The concentration of sodium lactate was sufficient to result in blood lactate levels which were within the range attained after maximum muscular exertion, or after the administration of adrenalin (Pitts, 1969). Thirteen of the 14 anxiety subjects developed anxiety attacks with the infusion of lactate. Only two of the 10 control subjects developed anxiety attacks.

This seemed a promising start, but the hypothesis that anxiety symptoms are simply due to excess lactate has not been supported by further studies. Not all patients with anxiety neurosis produce excess levels of lactate during exercise, nor is the excess production of lactate confined to patients with anxiety neurosis. Although the fact that lactate could exacerbate anxiety in anxiety-prone individuals was implied by the Pitts and McClure (1969) observations, it was not clear whether individuals are susceptible to this effect as a result of their anxiety neurosis, or whether special susceptibility to lactate contributes to the anxiety neurosis.

More recently Rifkin et al., (1981) produced panic attacks through the use of lactate infusion in nine patients with panic disorder. All nine patients were then treated with psychotherapy and a tricyclic antidepressant. Lactate infusion was repeated in six patients after they had been free of panic attacks for a minimum of one month. None of these patients suffered a panic attack during the second infusion. The difficulty of unequivocally specifying a biochemical basis for anxiety, even in the light of early promising results, is indicated by the lactate story. The current state of the lactate findings also warns us of the need for more research into the interaction between stress, stress-induced chemical changes, and the effects of the changes themselves upon mood.

5. Uric acid

The level of uric acid is generally elevated in people during demanding situations. This is so whether the demand is psychological, or if it is so-called 'stress' due to exercise. The uric acid is formed as a by-product of protein digestion—it is one of the ways that the body eliminates the excess nitrogen formed from protein metabolism. Uric acid is generally expelled through the urinary route; however, some is broken down to urea and ammonia. The urinary excretion of uric acid by human subjects can be increased by the elevation of the level of hormones of the adrenal cortex as well as by corticotropin. The fact that adrenal activity is involved with the changes in plasma uric acid levels, and in the rate of excretion, provides an expected link between uric acid and stress. This expectation is confirmed in practice.

The simplest summary would be that uric acid levels are elevated by stress. But, like so many simple summaries, there is a complex reality behind the uric acid response. A most interesting feature of the uric acid response is the specificity of the reaction. Uric acid levels seem to be very particular in the way they respond to both psychological stressors and physiological stressors. For example, after a similar workload of cycling or running, the level of uric acid response is more elevated and remains so for much longer in the case of the runners. When a so-called stress marker is not even constantly affected by two nominally similar forms of exercise, how can we expect to interpret its meaning in the wide range of different situations that are involved with stress in real life? The answer to this has not yet been offered but, not surprisingly, psychological differences in the response are beginning to be noticed as well.

Evidence of the rather poorly understood, but obviously important, specificity of the uric acid response has been noticed for many years. The elevation of levels of serum uric acid is highest during the anticipation phase of a potentially demanding situation, for example, in Army cadets immediately prior to the start of their first academic year (Clark *et al.*, 1975), or in factory workers when they are informed that their jobs will be terminated and the plant closed down (Kasl *et al.*, 1968). In an overview of the evidence relating to uric acid levels, it was concluded that this particular so-called stress marker was responsive not to the actual demands or stressfulness of a life event, but more to the *anticipation* of challenge, threat, or exposure to a stressor (Rahe *et al.*, 1982).

In some cases this anticipation might be associated with a greater preparedness, but this would of course depend upon the specific demands of the task and the resources available to the person anticipating the demands. In the case of the factory workers (Kasl *et al.*, 1968) those with the highest uric acid levels did not wait for the closure of the plant, but instead went out and found new jobs before their old ones were terminated. Whether or not this sort of adaptive activity is possible, and whether or not the stressor will be coped with, it would seem that the anticipation of demands leads to elevated levels of serum uric acid. It is also evident that there are personality differences which affect the levels of uric acid in the individual. This point is of interest to our understanding of the interactions between personality and endocrinology. But more important than this, the uric acid response is almost certainly linked with the onset and maintenance of a modern stress-related disease, repetition strain injury. This is dealt with in greater detail in Chapter 5.

C. A NEW SYNTHESIS OF PHYSIOLOGICAL AND PSYCHOLOGICAL RESPONSES

With the increased quantity and specificity of information relating the human physiological responses to stress, the possibility of a coherent story may appear to be growing more remote. The facts are quite at odds with the original proposition that stress is the response of the body to any demand, and that this response can be defined in terms of hormonal changes. There is continuing evidence that an activation of the pituitary-adrenal system is involved with the stress response, however, there is equally little doubt that the pattern of response is determined by the psychological processes of threat perception, evaluation, and coping.

The new primacy which must be given to the psychological processes need not mean that physiological measures have no value. Indeed this newly developing understanding provides a new perspective from which to interpret the biochemical data. The general proposition is that stress can alter the way the body functions, but the exact changes depend upon certain psychological factors. From this we are easily led to the idea of grouping the physiological responses according to psychological dimensions. This new approach promises to add a richness to the gestalt of the psychobiological understanding of human functioning. Already the factor structure of the endocrine response patterns has been linked to the psychological processes known to affect the stress response in humans. In one example of this composite approach, three psychoendocrine response factors were isolated (Vaernes *et al.*, 1982). These are:

a. A cortisol factor related to defence reactions;
b. A testosterone/prolactin factor related to role identifications; and
c. A catecholamine/growth hormone factor related to ideas about performance.

The experiment which yielded these relationships was innovative, and worthy of a brief description. The participants were United States Navy recruits who were non-swimmers. They were given two weeks to learn how to swim, then were required to pass a swimming test. The test required each recruit to jump from a 1.7 metre high platform into the deep end of a swimming pool, even if still they could not swim, and then attempt to float. If they could not float, they were pulled out of the pool by an instructor: 'Prior observations had indicated that this can be a very stressful experience for the non-swimmer... They were non-swimmers asked to swim and they were, so to speak, doomed to failure in the swimming pool. Defense mechanisms, as well as more complex strategies involving active cognitive acts reducing the threat, should therefore be of particular importance in this situation (Vaernes *et al.*, 1982, p. 125).

The participants in the study completed a number of psychological tests to determine their present levels of stress, their coping styles, and defensiveness. Blood and urine samples were also taken to enable analysis of stress-associated hormonal changes. Statistical analyses were carried out to assess which groupings of the hormonal changes coincided with individual differences in response to the stressful situation. As indicated above, three such factors were distinguished.

The need to validate these proposed psychophysiological factors will undoubtedly provide fertile ground for future research. The three factors suggested by Vaernes *et al.*, (1982) will be refined and reformulated. In the light of these developments our psychological definition of stress will probably need to be evaluated again. For the present, however, we will continue to discuss stress as a primarily psychological issue.

Chapter 4
PSYCHOLOGICAL MEASUREMENT OF STRESS

The measurement of a psychological mood state must be, in the end, related to psychological manifestations. This implies the need for a psychological measuring instrument. Various stress measures have been developed and used in experimental psychology and in clinical settings. Some of the many psychological tests used for measuring stress will be discussed here. A comprehensive review is not intended, nor is one necessary. There is an extraordinary degree of concordance among stress tests; they all appear to be measuring the one attribute. This concordance is indicated in many studies which compare one test with another.

There are two main reasons for measuring levels of stress. The first relates to clinical situations where the measurement of stress is intended to help the clinician in the development and evaluation of a stress management program. The second use of stress measures is when we are studying, or trying to control, the effects of stress upon performance.

The main point of this review will be to introduce examples of tests which satisfy one of these two areas. For the second application, that is, assessing stress and performance, there is a need to measure arousal at the same time as stress. Tests which enable this additional mood to be measured are relatively rare. The interpretation and use of combined stress and arousal deserves special attention since it is only when both are measured that any sense can be made of the effects of mood on performance.

The psychological assessment of stress assumes that people under stress will not only 'feel different' but that they will report these differences. In the psychological literature attending to feelings and the names applied to these feelings, one of the most durable 'feelings' is the concept of anxiety. Earlier, we noted that in present usage there is no clear distinction between anxiety and stress. Indeed, it is best to regard them as referring to the same construct. A review of psychological measurement of stress should therefore be expected to include measures which claim to gauge levels of anxiety.

A. TRAIT ANXIETY

When we talk about an anxious person, we sometimes mean that he or she is very likely to become anxious, or we may mean that the person is currently suffering from signs of stress. There is an important difference here. Spielberger's main contribution (Spielberger, et al., 1970) to the measurement of stress was to devise a scale which distinguished between these two aspects of stress. He called them Trait Anxiety, and State Anxiety. State Anxiety is, in effect, the same transient emotion that we have been referring to as 'stress' in this book. A person who scores high on Spielberger's State Anxiety scale is currently experiencing stress.

Trait Anxiety is somewhat different, and this difference was spelled out by Spielberger (Spielberger et al., 1970, p. 3): 'trait anxiety refers to relatively stable individual differences in anxiety proneness, that is to differences between people in the tendency to respond to situations perceived as threatening, with elevations in A-state intensity. As a psychological concept, trait anxiety has the characteristics of a class of constructs...[referred to as]... "behavioural dispositions" '.

In making the selection of a stress scale it is first important to decide whether it is the State or the general disposition, the Trait, which is of most interest. In some instances both would be important. In the clinical setting, patients generally complain of chronic stress. To evaluate the severity of their problem, and to provide a measure which might reflect the progress of therapy, it is often sensible to measure their general tendency to experience stress. In this case a trait scale is appropriate. In a research situation, or when we are interested in controlling the effects of stress on performance, then a State measure of stress must be used. It has already been shown that, where the relationship between stress and performance is of interest, arousal should be measured as well.

Spielberger developed his State/Trait Anxiety Scale (Spielberger *et al.*, 1970) to provide measures of both aspects of stress. The values obtained can be compared with established norms. Although these norms were developed upon a base of American (United States) people, comparable results have been obtained with other English speaking populations. Unpublished work by the authors has confirmed, for example, that Australian university students return essentially identical mean and standard deviations compared with those published by Spielberger *et al.*, (1970). Measurements made on subjects in the Australian business community again confirm the applicability of Spielberger's published norms for the 'general population' (e.g., Cornwall, 1983). Both of Spielberger scales have been widely used over the last decade. The State scale has been found to be particularly useful in monitoring stress levels in performance-stress studies, while the Trait scale has been used to indicate the likelihood or frequency of elevated stress levels.

Spielbergber's scales have become more or less accepted as the standard measures of anxiety or stress. The main criticism that could be made of Spielberger's State Anxiety scale, in the context of understanding stress-performance, is that it does not provide a measure of arousal. With the Trait Anxiety scale, a source of possible concern is that it contains many of the same items that are found on the State scale. Because of the item overlap, there could be interference between the responses a person makes on one scale if he or she has just completed the other. The difference between the State and the Trait scales is found in the form of the question: for State Anxiety, the person is asked about the *severity* of his or her feelings right now, while the Trait scale asks about the *frequency* of these feelings. To avoid this overlap of items, and possible interference between the two forms of the test, an alternative approach to the measurement of Trait Anxiety might be preferred. A widely accepted alternative to Trait Anxiety measurement is found in anxiety scales drawn from the Minnesota Multiphasic Personality Inventory (MMPI).

B. MINNESOTA MULTIPHASIC PERSONALITY INVENTORY TRAIT ANXIETY SCALES

Psychometric scales intended to measure trait anxiety include a series of (Minnesota Multiphasic Personality Inventory)-based scales. These trait anxiety measures have the advantage that, if the MMPI is given in a clinical setting as an aid to the diagnosis of psychological problems, then additional information about a person's tendency to experience stress is available without further testing being required.

One of the most widely used of these scales drawn from the items on the MMPI is the Manifest Anxiety Scale (MAS) (Dahlstrom *et al.*, 1976). The development of the MAS has been summarized by Graham (1977). Taylor (1953) devised the scale as an experimental measure to select subjects with high and low 'drive' in order to study the effects of drive on performance. The drive subject brought to the task was the level of his or her manifest anxiety. Five clinicians selected items from the MMPI, and a set of 50 anxiety items was agreed upon. The subsequent widespread use of this scale has enabled a number of generalizations to be made regarding the meaning of the scores. Subjects whose score on the MAS is high tend to perceive the environment as threatening and uncontrollable and they are less able than subjects whose score on the MAS is low to control autonomic reactions to stress situations. In stressful situations, the subject with a high score tends to feel anxious, tense and jumpy and is likely to experience some physiological changes such as excessive perspiration, increased pulse rate, and greater emotional discomfort.

The MAS scale was intended to produce a measure which would enable an interpretation of variations in performance. Despite this intention, the MAS is now regarded as a trait measure. Therefore, it may not correctly indicate the level of anxiety pertaining during the experimental situation. Although the level of anxiety indicated by the MAS may often predict the actual experienced level of anxiety, that is, the subject's level of stress, this may not always be so. It is therefore suggested that at least in experimental studies of the effects of stress or stressors on performance, there is a need to measure not the general propensity of an individual to respond to stressful situations, but the actual response of the person: 'the momentary level of a person's anxiety . . . cannot always be accurately forecast by means of pre-task MAS scores . . . high scores on MAS indicate a strong likelihood that subjects will respond to a wide variety of cues by becoming anxious . . . Therefore, it is necessary to know whether the anxiety proneness revealed by high MAS scores is actually being elicited by the stress-producing cues in the experiment. High MAS predictions may not be borne out in some studies because the high MAS subjects are not studied under high-stress conditions' (Dahlstrom *et al.*, 1975, p. 99).

It is possible that MMPI-based trait scales have an advantage over the Spielberger Trait anxiety scale. As mentioned above, the Spielberger Trait anxiety scale uses items which are the same or similar in form to those on the State form of the instrument. When both forms are to be used, the respondent may be to some extent influenced by his or her answers on the first-completed form. On the other hand, with the MMPI-based scales the items are quite different from those used in typical State stress scales, and thus there is little chance of the answer given to an MMPI-based trait scale interfering with the responses on a subsequent State instrument.

With the pressures of time which are faced by the psychological assessment profession, there has been a modern tendency to use abbreviated scales where possible. This has led to the development of a number of short forms of the MMPI. One of the most popular short forms of MMPI is the MMPI-168 (Overall *et al.*, 1975). The MMPI-168 uses only the first 168 items from the total 566 item inventory. When this form of the MMPI is used then Taylor's Manifest Anxiety Scale cannot be scored from the answer sets since the MAS questions are distributed over the entire 566 MMPI questions.

To allow the MAS to be retained as well as provide for the use of a shortened form of the MMPI, an equivalent form of MAS was devised. The 25 items on this new anxiety scale are distributed only among the first 168 questions of the MMPI, and therefore the new scale (which has been called the KAS) can be scored from this short form of the MMPI (King and Campbell, 1986). This new trait stress scale, KAS, has a correlation of 0.91 compared with the original MAS. The items on the KAS together with normative statistics, are given in Table 4.1.

C. THE LEEDS SCALES: ANXIETY AND DEPRESSION

It was indicated above that an appropriate measure of anxiety can indicate to the clinician the severity of a patient's condition. A second, and very important, reason for measuring psychological mood states is to help the clinician to decide exactly what is wrong with a patient. The clinical diagnosis of psychological problems is often poorly handled and in a later chapter we will develop this problem further in the section dealing with medication. For the present, let us accept that many patients may be wrongly diagnosed as suffering from a primary stress disorder when in fact their real problem is depression.

The overlap between stress and depression, and the source of the confusion in the differential diagnosis, can be more clearly understood if we direct our attention to the separable components of depression. From the many attempts which have been made to distinguish the components of depression, we have selected just one for review here. This is the Montgomery-Asberg Depression Scale (Montgomery and Asberg, 1979). This depression scale was selected because it has been accepted as being at least the equal of other respected scales in terms of its diagnostic power, but more than some others the Montgomery-Asberg scale is 'exclusively concerned with the psychic symptoms of depressive illness'—it does not focus attention on the psychomotor problems or the slowness of action which often accompany depression (Kearns *et al.*, 1982, p. 48). The ten domains which are tested in the Montgomery-Asberg scale are, in the words of its developers:

1. apparent sadness
2. reported sadness
3. inner tension
4. reduced sleep
5. reduced appetite
6. concentration difficulties
7. lassitude
8. inability to feel
9. pessimistic thoughts
10. suicidal thoughts

The third component of depression, 'inner tension', is scored by the interviewer over a six point scale:

0   placid, only fleeting inner tension
1
2   occasional feelings of edginess and illdefined discomfort
3
4   continous feelings of inner tension or intermittent panic which the patient can only master with some difficulty
5   unrelenting dread or anguish, overwhelming panic [Montgomery and Asberg, 1979, p. 387]
6

From this description of the components which combine to make up the depressive state, the feelings of dread, inner tension, or even panic will often be those about which the patient complains most. In the face of these complaints, the general clinician may find his or her attention deflected away from the additional problems—those which signal the presence of a primary depressive disorder.

The consequences of failing to diagnose depression in the first instance are perhaps not so grave when continuing psychotherapy is provided, but in a busy clinical situation many patients are given a medical prescription and little more attention than that. In Chapter 5, it is emphasized that antianxiety medication does not provide an effective treatment for depression. Therefore the busy medical practioner would be helped in his or her work if there were a simple and rapid assessment procedure which could distinguish between cases of primary depression and cases of stress. Such a test has been developed, and is called 'The Leeds Scales for Anxiety and Depression' (Snaith et al., 1976). It has the advantage of being a patient self-report test.

A simple self-rating instrument was developed in a clinically based development and validation procedure. The resulting instrument provides a separate score for Anxiety (stress in our terms) and Depression. The clinician

Table 4.1. The items on the MMPI-based trait stress scale KAS.

MMPI item number		Scoring response
3	I wake up fresh and rested most mornings.	F
10	There seems to be a lump in my throat much of the time.	T
13	I work under a great deal of tension.	T
21	At times I have very much wanted to leave home.	T
23	I am troubled by attacks of nausea and vomiting.	T
31	I have nightmares every few nights.	T
32	I find it hard to keep my mind on a task or job.	T
41	I have had periods of days, weeks, or months when I couldnt take care of things because I couldnt 'get going'.	T
43	My sleep is fitful and disturbed.	T
67	I wish I could be as happy as others seem to be.	T
72	I am troubled by discomfort in the pit of my stomach every few days or oftener.	T
76	Most of the time I feel blue.	T
82	I am easily downed in an argument.	T
86	I am certainly lacking in self-confidence.	T
94	I do many things which I regret afterwards (I regret things more often than others seem to).	T
102	My hardest battles are with myself.	T
106	Much of the time I feel as if I have done something wrong or evil.	T
107	I am happy most of the time.	F
125	I have a great deal of stomach trouble.	T
138	Criticism or scolding hurts me terribly.	T
142	I certainly feel useless at times.	T
147	I have often lost out on things because I couldnt make up my mind soon enough.	T
152	Most nights I go to sleep without thoughts or ideas bothering me.	F
158	I cry easily.	T
163	I do not tire easily.	F

F = false; T = true

is then guided in the formulation of a treatment program by comparing the two scores. The anxiety score is subtracted from the depression score, and, when the resulting difference is outside the range of -4 to $+4$, a clear diagnosis is obtained. For patients falling in between these two limits, further clinical evaluation would be recommended to determine the most appropriate course of action.

The value of the Leeds scales could, perhaps, be overstated. It is never a good idea to replace informed clinical evaluation with a psychometric test. There is always a real, statistical possibility that a diagnostic error could be made. However, as will be discussed later (Chapter 5), medical practitioners fail to correctly diagnose up to 90% of the cases of depression which they encounter. In the face of this record, a simple guide such as that offered by the Leeds scales should be invaluable in general medical practice. The items on the two scales, stress and depression, are as follows:

1. The differential diagnosis of anxiety and depression

The Leeds scales for the self-assesment of anxiety and depression comprise 22 items. When all items are answered, they provide both a diagnosis, (anxiety or depression), and a measure of the severity of the disorder. The present discussion attends just to the differentiation of the two disorders. The response is on a four point scale: 'definitely' (3), 'sometimes' (2), 'not much' (1) and 'not at all' (0).

The items relating to stress are:

I get very frightened or panic feelings for apparently no reason at all.
I am restless and can't keep still.
I feel anxious when I go out of the house alone.
I am more irritable than usual.
I feel scared or frightened.
I get palpitations, or a sensation of 'butterflies' in my stomach or chest.

The items relating to depression are:

I feel miserable and sad.
I still enjoy things I used to (*negative scoring*).
I have lost interest in things.
I wake early and then sleep badly for the rest of the night.
I have a good appetite (*negative scoring*).
I feel life is not worth living.

D. MEASURING STATE STRESS AND AROUSAL

It is indicated at other places in this book that at least two different mood state responses can occur due to a perceived demand. These two responses were labelled stress and arousal. Although these two moods are distinct psychologically, they correspond to aspects of biophysiological changes which overlap to some extent. The evidence which points to the distinction between stress and arousal is substantial, but the separation of the two constructs has often been ignored in the development of psychological measures of the stress. For example, Spielberger *et al.*, (1970, p. 3) described their concept of State anxiety as including not only feelings of tension and apprehension, but also 'heightened autonomic nervous system activity'. This reference to autonomic nervous activity sounds as though it refers to that part of the response which we have called arousal. The *description* by Spielberger *et al.*, (1970) of what they were trying to measure could easily lead to confusion, but despite this problem the actual scale itself has always been accepted as measuring anxiety or stress.

E. THE STRESS/AROUSAL CHECK LIST MEASURE OF STRESS AND AROUSAL

Attending to the difficulty of distinguishing between stress and arousal, Cox and his coworkers developed an adjective check list which produced two factors labelled stress and arousal (Mackay *et al.*, 1978). Cox's Stress/Arousal Adjective Check List (SACL) was initially based upon the responses of a sample of British university students. Further studies by Cox (Cox *et al.*, 1977) which show within-subject differences due to exposure to stressors have supported the validity of the two factors.

The background to the development of the SACL is of interest here, not just for historical reasons, but also because it sheds light upon some alternative approaches to mood state measurement which is discussed below. The starting point for the SACL was a group of items which were claimed to show four different styles of arousal or 'activation' (Thayer, 1967). Notice that, at this stage, Thayer avoided the more familiar descriptors such as stress, anxiety or arousal for his factors. The evidence that Thayer's scales did in fact refer to what we generally call 'stress' and 'arousal' came from later refinements in his work. Two of the four styles of arousal were associated with an increase in this activation: *general activation* and *high activation*. The other two were associated with a reduction in their particular types of activation: *general deactivation* and *deactivation-sleep*. This work has been criticized on a number of grounds, but at the same time has been noted in most modern developments of the measurement of mood. The most immediately obvious criticism is the lack of meaning in the names which Thayer selected for his four factors. The second, and most common, criticism lies in the fact that the same, or very similar, words can be easily grouped into just two factors - and these two factors seem to make sense. One of them extends from general activation, with its connotations of a pleasurable state of elevated arousal, to deactivation-sleep which is defined by descriptors like drowsy, sleepy, and tired. The other factor which can be drawn from Thayer's work is obtained by combining high activation with deactivation (Russel, 1980). The resulting two-factor solution is interpretable, particularly when labels such as 'arousal' and 'stress', respectively, are applied to them. Cox's SACL is an example of a useful two-factor solution to Thayer's 'activation' studies.

The SACL has been further studied in a wider range of contexts on

Australian subjects (King *et al.*, 1983). The original Cox scale had 34 items, comprising 20 stress items and 14 arousal items. When the strongest of these items were selected to make a scale with 10 stress and 10 arousal items, a factor structure similar to that of the longer SACL was reported. The form of the 20 item SACL is given in Table 4.2. Normative statistics follow this section. The scales obtained from the shorter version of SACL are so closely related with the values on the longer form that no psychometric advantage can be attributed to either the short or the long form. The two stress scales have a correlation coefficient of 0.96, and the two arousal scales also have the same correlation, 0.96.

The SACL has been further investigated on a range of Australian subjects and the results have indicated that the scales are sufficiently robust that they may be confidently taken from one English-speaking population to another without significant changes to the psychometrics. Not only did the two factorially derived scales retain their orthogonality, but the real world meaning of the two scales was clarified: '. . . arousal may be regarded as a useful or appropriate aspect of the response to a perceived demand. Arousal was elevated in response to a high load cognitive demand, and was at its lowest among psychiatric patients. . . Stress was. . . associated with perceived threat combined with a diminished belief in one's ability to cope. . .' (King *et al.*, 1983, p. 478).

In considering the use of either the longer (Cox *et al.*, 1978) or the shorter (King *et al.*, 1983) version of the SACL, it should be remembered that both stress and, particularly, arousal are regarded as volatile mood states. For example, it was shown that speeded pencil and paper tests had a marked effect on arousal, usually elevating the score (King *et al.*, 1983). It was therefore suggested that, because of the volatility of the mood state, the testing procedure might itself interact with the parameter which it purports to measure. If this is borne in mind it is reasonable to conclude that a test procedure should be as short as possible, within the limitations of satisfactory statistical validity, in order to minimize possible test-induced interference.

1. Normative statistics for the 20 item stress/arousal adjective check list

Scoring

Stress Scale
score one point if "?" or "−" on items 1,2,5,14
score one point if " + + " or " + " on items 7,10,11,13,18,20
Arousal Scale
score one point if "?" or "−" on items 8,12,15,19
score one point if " + + " or " + " on items 3,4,6,9,16,17

Table 4.2. Mood state questionnaire (Stress/Arousal Check List).

Please answer each of the following questions according to how you feel *right now*.
Answer each item by marking the response to indicate:
if the answer is
Definitely yes   + +
Slightly yes   +
Not sure *or*
don't understand   ?
Definitely not   −

1.	calm	+ +	+	?	−	11.	uptight	+ +	+	?	−
2.	contented	+ +	+	?	−	12.	drowsy	+ +	+	?	−
3.	active	+ +	+	?	−	13.	tense	+ +	+	?	−
4.	vigorous	+ +	+	?	−	14.	relaxed	+ +	+	?	−
5.	comfortable	+ +	+	?	−	15.	passive	+ +	+	?	−
6.	lively	+ +	+	?	−	16.	energetic	+ +	+	?	−
7.	uneasy	+ +	+	?	−	17.	alert	+ +	+	?	−
8.	tired	+ +	+	?	−	18.	bothered	+ +	+	?	−
9.	aroused	+ +	+	?	−	19.	sleepy	+ +	+	?	−
10.	worried	+ +	+	?	−	20.	distressed	+ +	+	?	−

Now please place a cross (X) to indicate your position along the two lines below.
Respond as you feel *right now*.
comfortable
or calm _____ *worried*

active _____ *sleepy*

stress mean and standard deviation: 1.7, 2.0
arousal mean and standard deviation: 7.3, 2.2

F. THE PROFILE OF MOOD STATES SCALES: TENSION AND VIGOR

The Profile of Mood States (POMS) is a 65 item adjective check list. In the
development of the POMS, a wide range of adjectives was considered. The
words were chosen to provide a cover of many possible human moods. The
developers included words which allowed for the possibility of a mood which
might be called 'cheerful', yet distinct from one which might be called 'friendly',
or another called 'depressed'. From the originally extensive list of words there
were indications of six mood states which were stable, and which regularly
appeared to be present in different groups of people (McNair *et al.*, 1981). The
six scales have been called:

Tension-Anxiety
Depression-Dejection
Anger-Hostility
Vigor-Activity
Fatigue-Inertia
Confusion-Bewilderment.

The POMS scales were steadily refined over a series of analyses of answers from a variety of people. The people tested included groups of 'normal' college students, and patients at a psychiatric clinic. The people used in the developmental and validatory studies were all from the United States of America. The fact that the work for the POMS only used English-speaking people in the USA does not mean that the six POMS moods are found only in the United States of America. The universality of the POMS scales has been demonstrated in a study of a set of Swedish mood adjectives. Successive analyses led to the pregressive refinement of six quite similar factors (Bohlin and Kjellberg, 1973; 1975). The English titles given to these Swedish factors were: Stress (compares with Tension); Irritation (compares with Anger); Energy (compares with Vigor); Sleep–Wakefulness (compares with Fatigue); Concentration (compares with Confusion); and Euphoria, which probably presents the bipolar opposite of Depression.

The most immediately relevant question for us is whether or not the POMS provides a measure of stress. From a consideration of the names given to the scales, it is evident that the first scale, Tension–Anxiety, may be a candidate stress scale. This expectation is confirmed by a number of the studies presented by the POMS authors (McNair et al., 1981). For example, when the POMS items are completed in accord with the instructions to respond 'how you have been feeling during the past week including today', a correlation of 0.80 with the MAS (reviewed above) was obtained (McNair et al., 1981). In this sense the POMS can give an estimate of trait stress. Other comparisons are also presented in the same source, and all confirm the proposition that the Tension–Anxiety scale is indeed a measure of the construct generally recognized as anxiety or stress. Given this concordance, it seems a pity that the developers of the POMS did not use either 'anxiety' or 'stress' as the label for this scale.

The POMS scales which seem to parallel the idea of arousal are the fourth and fifth, Vigor-Activity, and Fatigue–Inertia. These two labels are reminiscent of Thayer's positive and negative scales: those which were forced into the bipolar arousal factor by Cox and his colleagues (Mackay et al., 1978). Both Vigor and Fatigue contain only unipolar items, that is Vigor has only items such as 'lively', while Fatigue has only items such as 'worn out'. There are no comparisons with other measures of the arousal construct provided in the POMS manual (McNair et al., 1981). This deficiency is probably in part because of the relatively limited degree of attention that the literature has paid to the psychological measurement of arousal.

Although the POMS separates the arousal domain into two components, Vigor and Fatigue, the Vigor scale alone has been found by us to correspond with the concept of arousal reasonably well. The items on the Fatigue scale seem to represent a state which is at once low in arousal, but at the same time includes some of the negative emotions of higher stress. That is, Fatigue on the POMS seems to indicate that the person is not only low in energy, but is also feeling bad about it. Fatigue is therefore partly related to arousal, and partly related to stress, as we have come to understand it. It is therefore suggested that, for a measurement of stress and arousal which corresponds to the ideas developed in this book, the Vigor scale should be used to represent arousal. The disadvantage of using the Vigor scale is that it does not include the balance of negative words which are needed for a full range of the idea of arousal.

Whether or not the POMS has the ability to fully represent Arousal has been discussed by the developers of the test, Lorr and McNair (1984). They have recently produced a new Bipolar form of the POMS which has just one scale to indicate the dimension of arousal. This new scale is called Energetic-Tired.

1. Stress and the other profile of mood state scales

An important advantage of use of the POMS is that, in addition to tapping the stress–arousal domain, the POMS simultaneously provides a measure of other mood states. These other moods, especially anger and depression, can be clinically relevant to understanding the experience of anxiety. Where a diagnostic decision between a primary problem of anxiety, or of depression, is the question, then it is suggested that the Leeds Scale should be used, since this scale was specifically designed for the purpose of making that distinction. But the POMS has some special contributions to make as well.

A valuable clinical use of the POMS is that relationships between the different POMS scales can give the clinician a better overall view of the effects that stress has on a person's life. For example, after a day of tension and stress, one person may be very fatigued and weak (low on Vigor and/or high on Fatigue) while another person may become angry. A patient may be referred for psychological help mainly because of his or her chronic anxiety problems, but the underlying cause may be associated with anger or depressive feelings. The relationships between these other negative moods and stress can be uncovered by asking the patient to fill out a series of POMS questionnaires, for instance, one form for each day of the week.

The analysis of these repeat measures is best conducted using a computer program designed for the purpose. Such a program can be easily written for most personal computers, or one may be available from a software supplier specializing in psychology. The measures which analysis of repeated administrations can yield are:

a. Individual scores on the six scales for each day.
b. Average scores on each of the six scales over the week.
c. The variability or volatility of the person on each of the scales.
d. The relationships (correlations) between the scales.

Of these four measures, volatility is often the most informative. This can be measured, for example, by computing the standard deviation of each scale over the week. For most of the scales there is typically little change on a day-to-day basis, but one or two scales may fluctuate greatly. Having noticed the most variable mood(s), the clinician can then draw the client's attention to the possible underlying source of the problem. This procedure is particularly valuable when dealing with patients referred for 'anxiety' problems, when the real problem is poorly controlled anger. They often do not understand their negative moods, and the analysis can help to make the causes clearer to them.

The value of this analysis is best illustrated by an example. A patient was referred for psychological help, from a general practitioner, with the following note:

Dear Doctor,

May I refer Mr E, 28 years old fitter and turner who has recurrent *tension headaches*. He wanted some help with this and I advised him to see you for this rather than prescribe sedatives.

TREATMENT: The client was asked to complete one POMS form each day. The results indicated that two scales were much more volatile than the others. The most volatile scales were Anger and Vigor.

The matrix of correlations between all scales was computed and the two correlations of greatest clinical relevance showed that the Anger scale had a correlation of 0.86 with the Tension scale; Vigor and Anger were also fairly strongly associated with a correlation coefficient of 0.71.

It was pointed out to the patient that his tension headaches were probably connected with feelings of low energy and with outbursts of anger. Therapy based around anger management principles followed, with a rapid decline in the incidence of tension headaches.

By reporting this case we intend to illustrate that rapid insight into a patient's condition can be obtained by the use of repeated POMS measures, combined with an appropriate analysis. Specific patient management techniques are dealt with in Chapter 5.

A possible disadvantage with the POMS is that the total of 65 items must be responded to, and the stress items are distributed throughout the form. Where repeated measures over the course of a research experiment, or speed of completion, is important this number of items may be regarded as excessive. The size of the POMS would obviously be more of a disadvantage when only stress and arousal are of interest. This problem of length has now been attended to, and a shorter form of the POMS has been suggested (Shacham, 1983). This shortened form uses only 37 of the original 65 items. The scales from the short form of the POMS are excellent estimates of the original scales with correlation coefficients all greater than 0.95.

The six POMS scales were derived through the technique of factor analysis. That is, the six scales were, by definition, independent of each other or uncorrelated. This absence of correlation between the scales was found from analysis of the responses of many different people. The above analysis showed something quite different. The case of Mr E demonstrated that, for a particular individual, there might be a strong pattern of association between the scales, and that this association can have important implications about the way a person is reacting to life.

G. THE INDEPENDENCE OF STRESS AND AROUSAL

In discussing stress and arousal thus far, it has always been emphasized that the two moods are independent. This is supported by work from a number of studies which found independent factors representing stress and arousal. It is supported by the persistence of a near-zero correlation between accepted measures of stress and arousal. It is supported by our theoretical understanding of what these two moods indicate with regard to people's reactions to life. By our use of the term 'independent factors' we mean that simply to know the level of stress tells us nothing about the level of arousal. People with high stress may be highly aroused, or they may feel very flat, lifeless and devoid of resources—either of these alternatives could be encountered, and in fact the independence of stress and arousal guarantees that examples of both will occur. The independence holds true, on average, with a large group of people. But what about individual people?

We can all think of someone who gets highly excited, very active—in short, aroused—whenever he or she is stressed. That is to say, we would be able to predict that high arousal will coincide with high stress for that person. We can all think of a person who generally loses all initiative and vigor under the effects of stress. This too is an enduring characteristic of that particular person. This means that the 'independence' of stress and arousal would not be expected for individual people. This can be shown when a group of people fill in a stress and arousal questionnaire on each of seven successive days. The results are not surprising. Some people have a consistent negative relationship between stress and arousal; high stress means low arousal for them. Others (not so many of them) have a positive relationship with high stress being associated with high arousal.

The relationship between stress and arousal can be expressed as a correlation coefficient. This was illustrated in the search for relationships among the six POMS scales. The independence of stress and arousal can be given a more interpretable meaning if the two moods are represented as two lines at right angles to each other—that is what a correlation of zero means. But we have just established that the two moods may not be independent for a particular person; the two lines may be at some angle other than 90 degrees. The cosine of this angle is of course equal to the correlation coefficient. Some people will have a positive association between stress and arousal, indicated by an angle less than 90 degrees. For some, high stress will be associated with low arousal, and this negative relationship will be indicated by an angle which is between 90 and 180 degrees. To illustrate the spread of the angles between stress and arousal, the data for the soccer players (experiment 2.2 in Chapter 2) are given in Table 4.3.

A point of interest coming from this new way of expressing a person's stress and arousal variations is that the angle indicates a somewhat stable tendency; different people respond with a particular pattern of stress and arousal. That is, there seems to be a type of 'behavioural disposition' as Spielberger put it (Spielberger *et al.*, 1970). A point of practical interest is that the angle between stress and arousal provides the basis for a distinction to be made between sports performers, at the top level, and more 'normal' people. It showed those who perform better under stress. This distinction, and what it means, will be discussed in Chapter 6.

The use of angles to represent the relationship between stress and arousal is not a new idea. In fact it has been shown that the six or so moods which are distinguished by the POMS and other similar studies can be placed around the circumference of a circle. This circular distribution of moods means that just two primary dimensions can be used to define all moods (Russell, 1980). One of these two primary dimensions was defined by the descriptors 'arousal' and 'sleepy', while the other defined the 'pleasure–displeasure dimension' (Russell, 1980, p. 1163). Russell used a variety of scaling techniques to show the average position of the different moods around a circle and in each case the circle could be defined by the two dimensions that we have come to recognize as stress and arousal. The first important point to come from Russell's work was that, on average, all other moods can be fitted into a two-dimensional space which is defined by stress and arousal.

The second point which comes from Russell's scaling studies was that he presented evidence of individual differences in the location of the different moods, and individual differences in the angle between stress and arousal. Although stress and arousal were, on average, orthogonal, Russell's data support the proposal developed in this book; that the angle between these two moods varies for different individuals. Russell did not elaborate on the meaning of the range of angles for different people, but the data he presented made it clear that if the arousal diameter (aroused to sleepy) is fixed, then for most

Table 4.3. The angle between stress and arousal for individuals.

Player number	Cosine	Angle
1	.29	73
2	−.75	139
3	−.47	118
4	.50	60
5	−.87	150
6	−.37	112
8	.29	73
9	.17	80
10	−.66	131
11	−.36	111
12	−.16	99
13	−.78	141
14	−.32	109
15	−.55	123
16	−.50	120
17	−.31	108

of his individuals the location of the stress diameter (defined by pleasure or contented to distress or misery) was distributed over the range 45° to 135°. This range is quite similar to the more exact data given for the soccer players in Table 4.3.

In summary, the actual level of a person's stress and arousal should be measured before it is possible to predict likely effects of either mood upon performance. The two moods are, on average, independent which means that to know the value of one does not provide knowledge of the level of the other. But for some individual people there is a consistent trend for the two moods to change in unison. This range of individual differences has been established by other studies, but has not previously been used or measured. This book provides a method of measuring an individual's stress–arousal relationship through the use of repeated measures. Later, in Chapter 6, the importance of this angle between stress and arousal will be raised.

H. VERY SHORT STRESS TESTS

In some instances it may be difficult to obtain a complete set of answers to a pencil and paper inventory. Such cases could occur when the person under study is involved with a time-demanding task, or when he or she is preoccupied with some pressing issue—perhaps even the stressor situation itself. The initial motivation for the shortening of the 34 item SACL was such a situation (King *et al.*, 1983). It was found that novice parachutists awaiting their first jump became edgy and complained when filling out the 34 item test. They often said that all the words were the same, or that the test was too long. Subsequent work with a similar group of novice parachutists using the 20 item scale did not elicit complaints about the test. However, in some cases, for example when testing sports participants during a short break in a match, even the 20 item scale would be too long.

Very short tests of stress have been developed and used in the past. An example of a rapid if rather informal measure which was subsequently regarded as 'stress' used the response on a five point scale anchored at either end by 'not much to do' and 'too much to do' (Rahe et al., 1982). Intuitively such a scale does not seem to clearly distinguish between stress and other mood states, or even non-emotional evaluations of the expected work load.

A more systematic development of a scale for making immediate stress estimates has been undertaken by the writers. This new short stress and arousal scale is based upon Cox's SACL, (Mackay et al., 1978) reviewed above. For each item on the Cox SACL, the loading on the parent factor, and also the mean response rate was known (King et al., 1983). The response rate indicated the strength of the item, while the factor loading indicated the purity of each item with regard to the parent factor. From these data it was possible to select two items from the stress scale such that one appeared to be placed at the extreme upper end of the stress dimension and the other was at the lower end. These two items could then be validly regarded as anchoring a unidimensional construct. Similarly with arousal, two items were selected, after considering factor loadings and item response rates, to define the arousal dimension.

These items were selected to define a 10 centimetre line, anchored at either end by the stress or arousal words. This line was to provide a linear measure of the person's mood state (see Table 4.2). The results of this linear measure could then be compared with the 20 item SACL. The results of this comparison show that the two linear measures retained the orthogonality of the original factors; the stress line was not significantly correlated with either the arousal scale nor with the arousal line. Similarly the arousal line was not significantly correlated with the stress scale nor with the stress line. The correlations between the arousal line and arousal scale was 0.83, and between the stress scale and the stress line, 0.83. The lines are illustrated at the foot of the 20 item SACL illustrated in Table 4.2. The mean values for them are as follows:

Stress line 4.5 cm (from left), SD 2.6 cm
Arousal line 5.1 cm (from right), SD 2.7 cm

The statistical validity of the Linear Arousal and Stress Scale (LASS) was indicated by the comparison with the parent SACL scores. A further test of the validity of the two scales can be made by comparing the selected polar items with the mood descriptors arranged, on average, around Russell's circular distribution of moods. One of Russell's primary dimensions was always defined by 'arousal', which inevitably found 'sleepy' located diametrically opposite. This is in agreement with the present LASS arousal line. The orthogonal stress dimension on Russell's model was described by Russell as a 'pleasure–displeasure' dimension. It is not immediately clear whether this is identical with what we have called stress, but in an earlier discussion of this pleasure–displeasure dimension, Russell indicated that it was 'found to account for almost all of the reliable variance in a sample of commonly used scales of affect [including]...anxiety' (Russell, 1979, p. 354). Words like 'comfortable', 'calm', 'pleasure', or 'content' described the positive end of this mood, while 'distress' and 'misery' defined the negative pole. These words are quite comparable with the LASS items. Also of comparative interest is a study which investigated arousal-related items. In a factorially derived grouping of positive and negative pairs of words (Mehrabian and Russell, 1971) one of the domains distinguished was labelled 'arousal'. Unfortunately they did not seek to measure 'stress'. The word pairs defining this arousal domain included two items which were quite similar to those used by the present authors to define the 'arousal' line for the LASS, that is alert–sleepy, on the LASS compared with wide awake–sleepy (Mehrabian and Russell, 1971).

In summary, the rapid measurement of stress and arousal can be achieved with an instrument such as that described above: the LASS. Work to support this instrument has been previously published, but has not led to the formal development of a similar instrument. Studies using the LASS have been conducted by the writers. One such study is presented in Chapter 2. The results indicate that a reliable and meaningful measure of the two target moods is obtained.

For an extension of the studies of mood and performance, a Finnish language version of the LASS was developed. Its use is briefly described in Chapter 6. The items which define the Finnish LASS, and its normative statistics, are given as follows:

Stress line
rauhallinen . . . *huolestunut*, mean 3.6, SD 2.7 cm (from left)

Arousal line
väsynyt . . . *aktiivinen*, mean 6.1, SD 2.9 cm (from left)
(based on responses of 117 Finnish people).

Chapter 5
CLINICAL CONTROL OF STRESS

Anxiety, or stress, occupies an important place in all theories of psychology. All theories are in agreement in predicting that all humans are capable of experiencing stress under particular circumstances. They all also predict that the differences in individual responses can be understood in the way that the environment is interpreted. But despite this overall agreement, quite different ideas have been presented to explain how these individual differences occur.

With regard to the clinical management of stress, we are interested in the fact that stress affects performance, and how we can alter the effects of the stress response in our lives.

Naturally, there are individual differences in the level of inappropriate anxiety which people feel and it is worth remembering that much of psychoanalytic theory, and also the ideas of other approaches to therapy, are based upon studies of the few excessively anxious people who present for psychological help. This concentration by theorists upon the fragile few is fine if the resulting theories are to be applied in a clinical setting, but the pronouncements may be less useful in understanding the effects of stress on the more robust majority. The use and control of stress in this latter group, that is 'normal' people, is dealt with in the final chapter.

From the study of physiology, we could not escape the conclusion that stress is psychological. Stress is caused by the way we think about ourselves and our environment. The theories which will be of most intterest to us will therefore be those which deal with the thoughts people have, especially under threatening situations. There are of course plenty of theories which relate to how people think, but for the present we will consider ideas from just two quite different sources.

The first source is psychoanalysis. Psychoanalysis has always been fascinating to the lay person, and its mention generally causes at least an indication of interest from professionals, too. Part of its fascination no doubt stems from the obscure style of its pronouncements, part from the fact that psychoanalysis deals with the unknowable recesses of our subconscious mind, and part perhaps because it has become almost an obsession for 'modern' psychologists to dismiss almost anything that can be linked to Freud. Together, these attitudes to psychoanalysis provide the ingredients which are bound to make a topic perennially interesting; that is, it is a mysterious and controversial subject which just might help us to understand more about ourselves. Those aspects of psychoanalytic theory presented here are not all that controversial. They relate to the type of belief systems—the group of thoughts—that help to prevent the development of stress.

The second source is the Rational Emotive Therapy (RET) of Albert Ellis (1975). RET outlines the beliefs that cause or elevate stress. The ideas of RET are shared with other modern cognitive therapies (that is, therapies which attend to people's problems by encouraging realistic thinking). RET was chosen because it most clearly singles out and describes typical stress-producing beliefs.

A. PSYCHOANALYTICAL VIEWS OF STRESS

When considering psychoanalysis it seems historically appropriate to begin with Freud. He proposed that in infancy a person experiences both the physiological and the psychological components of anxiety (stress) when he or she feels the threat of separation from a source of comfort. This response becomes more general as the person grows. In adult life the same type of separation anxiety, originating from the birth trauma, is experienced in the face of any threat. Sometimes this anxiety is appropriate, but sometimes it is excessive and is of no value at all.

Freud proposed the existence of separate components of the mind. These parts include the infantile, primitive, emotional, self-centred 'id', and the more rational 'ego'. The id cannot estimate situations of danger but when it becomes aware of a threat, processes initiated or executed in the id cause the ego to develop anxiety. There is a tendency for the ego to restrict the development of anxiety to a minimum. In personally threatening situations the anxiety is often reduced by action for dealing with or avoiding the danger. Thus anxiety serves to give a warning of danger and stimulates the institution of some physical means of averting danger. On the other hand when the anxiety-provoking thoughts cannot be reduced by avoiding a situation then the psychological defences of repression and denial are likely to be used. These defences aim to prevent conscious (ego) awareness of the danger by distorting the person's interpretations of reality.

The excessive or habitual use of psychological defences is often associated with neurosis, but the use of psychological defences is not restricted to abnormal or neurotic patients. There is a special class of defences, the 'narcissistic defences', which develop throughout childhood and in later life enable adults to survive without a morbid fixation on the inevitability of their own deaths. Shaw (1983) has reviewed three of these narcissistic defences. Like other psychological defences, each of the three is contrary to the real experience and logic of the situation. They are therefore to some extent fragile and when undermined they can greatly interfere with a person's ability to continue in normal life.

The first narcissistic defence is: *I am invulnerable and immortal*. As infants none of us is able to conceive of his or her own death, and this residual infantile narcissism underlies many manifestly risky acts which are committed by school children, adolescents, and some adults. Relevant to this belief is the relationship between exercise and stress. The importance of physical fitness and regular exercise as a way of preventing stress comes up time and time again. From a psychoanalytical stance it could be suggested that part of the value of exercise in reducing stress may be that the delusion of invulnerability is strengthened by each success over difficult physical challenges.

The second narcissistic defence is: *The delusion of the omnipotent servant*. This defence is based upon the fact that once we had all-powerful servants in the form of our parents. They were really big in those days. They protected us in seemingly impossible situations. They satisfied all of our wants and needs. Their wisdom was unquestioned or at least unquestionable.

The third defence is: *The belief in group support*. In the first instance we learned to trust our caregivers, especially the mother figure, for support. Later in childhood and during adolescence this trust in another turns to the expectation of peer support. In adult life this expectation of, and demand for, peer support is transformed into the concept of community support and approval. The perception that we have community support is taken as evidence that in adversity everyone will pull together. Intermittent reinforcement of this expectation of succour and support from others in our group is provided. Examples of support are strongly publicized during and after natural disasters such as earthquakes, volcanoes, floods and bushfires. The post-traumatic neuroses (especially chronic anxiety) that appear between six months and one year after a major disaster coincide with the disintegration of the immediate network of community support. After about six months, the individual's plight is no longer newsworthy or vote catching, and therefore the traumatized people steadily lose faith in the second defence—belief in helpful leaders. As anxiety develops, belief in group support also fails under the increasing weight of evidence that no-one really cares.

In Chapter 6, we will see how the undermining of these belief systems in the workplace can lead to stress. We shall also see how it is possible to maintain or strengthen psychological defences, and thus provide a barrier against the incidence of an epidemic of worker stress.

B. RATIONAL EMOTIVE VIEWS OF STRESS

The narcissistic defences are a set of beliefs which are to some extent out of step with reality. They are by definition irrational, but they appear to provide a useful barrier against stress according to psychoanalytic theory (Shaw, 1983). Similar irrational beliefs are described by Albert Ellis (1975) but in his Rational Emotive Therapy (RET) model these irrational beliefs are the cause of stress.

As with other theories, the RET view is that the experience of stress is related to the individual's appraisal of the balance between available resources and situational demands. The special contribution of RET to our understanding of stress has been concentration upon the self-statements which lead to excessive stress. These self-statements are 'irrational' meaning that they are either totally out of step with reality, or that they are an unnecessary exaggeration of the real situation. But the beliefs which have been singled out by RET are not only irrational, they are also irresistable to many people. These disruptive, stress-producing beliefs generally include a strongly held view about how things 'should' be.

Thirteen major classes of irrational beliefs have been described by Albert Ellis (1976). This collection of beliefs was based upon Ellis' experience with thousands of patients. The following list, drawn from RET writings, does not pretend to cover all irrational beliefs and it is often the task of the therapist to decide where the client's beliefs fit in with this list and then to demonstrate to the client the validity of the therapist's decision.

1. I must be loved and approved of by everybody.
2. When people behave unfairly they must be punished: 'They' should not be allowed to do that.
3. It's awful when things are not the way I'd like them to be.
4. I should be very anxious about events that are uncertain or potentially dangerous.

5. I am not worthwhile unless I am competent, adequate, and achieving things: I absolutely must succeed this time.
6. I have got to find the perfect solution to this problem.
7. The world should be fair and just: I deserve better treatment.
8. I should be comfortable and without pain at all times: I shouldn't be upset at this time.
9. I must be going crazy.
10. It is easier to try to avoid life's difficulties.
11. I need someone strong to depend upon at all times: Other people should take care of me.
12. Emotional misery comes from external pressures.
13. My past is the cause of my present problems, and so there is nothing I can do about things: Because I have failed in the past I will always continue to fail.

Some hint of these irrational beliefs is present in everyone's thinking and evaluation processes, but when the beliefs start to dominate reality, anxiety mounts. A snowballing effect tends to take place at this stage. The first consequence of entertaining an irrational belief about the way the world 'should' be is that the believer notices the unpleasant nature of the developing emotion, stress. A second series of irrational beliefs then comes into action. These beliefs hinge upon the notion that 'I can't stand this frustration', and 'these awful feelings are more than I can stand', and then lead to either the anger response 'it is "their" fault that things are so bad' or self-condemnation in the form of 'these feelings prove that I am an absolutely worthless sort of person'.

When these irrational beliefs take over the person's thoughts it is easy to see that performance on any task will be disrupted. The reader has probably recognized some of these irrational beliefs—they are held by many of our colleagues with religious reverence. The thoughts can be refuted but the disputing process needs the skill of an experienced therapist. As indicated above, these thoughts are compellingly attractive to many people, and once a person is suffering from the resulting stress there is little hope for rational self-help.

C. PREVENTING AND OVERCOMING STRESS

Now that we have covered a little background theory about the thinking patterns that prevent or cause stress we are in a position to use this information in real-life situations and in the clinical situation. By 'the clinical situation', we usually mean the treatment of people who are seriously or continually stricken by stress. The underlying cause of the stress, the special forces which have eroded the patient's defences, and the current conflicts which provide a focus for irrational thoughts all need special individual attention. It is for this reason that there are so many different approaches to stress management. Each approach is successful in certain clinical instances: none is universally useful. The task is always the same: to overcome the negative thinking processes which convince the patient that he or she cannot 'cope', and to rebuild robust defences. We will summarize the main clinical approaches, and indicate some of the problems which are typically matched to these methods. This is not intended as a self-help menu. Stress necessarily disrupts the evaluation procedures and this consequence makes the problem of clinical levels of stress quite unsuitable for self-help.

1. Hypnosis/Relaxation

It is a common observation that people under stress are 'tense'. This tension refers to some sense of emotional tension as well as manifest physical tension. Hypnotic techniques usually involve a physical relaxation procedure as part of the trance induction process. Physical relaxation itself can have significant effects in reducing some of the symptoms of stress. It is an opportunity to focus the mind on something other than negative thoughts. It provides a task at which the patient can, with appropriate guidance, succeed. Because of these distraction processes, physical relaxation can lead the exhausted patient to a stage where sleep is possible. The elimination of sleep difficulties can be an important part of the total process of stress management, so we will briefly consider the connections between stress and sleep.

Insomnia ranks third behind the common cold and headaches as a reason for seeking professional aid. Although sleep difficulties do not necessarily mean that a person is suffering from stress, about one third of sleeping problems are believed to be due to psychological factors (Fuerst, 1983). In a study of 25 insomniacs who were recruited through a newspaper advertisement, it was found that the poor sleepers had elevated levels of neuroticism and stress, as indicated by Minnesota Multiphasic Personality Inventory (MMPI) scales: 'Insomniacs thus appear to be more neurotic, anxious, and worried than their normal counterparts' (Freedman and Sattler, 1982, p. 387). And the role of stress in insomnia was also emphasized in a comprehensive review of the disorder: 'A large number of insomnias are due to intrusive, relatively uncontrollable, cognitive activity, especially what might be best labelled as worry' (Borkovec, 1982, p. 890).

There is a tendency to assume that relaxation treatments are the therapy of choice in dealing with sleep disturbance, whether or not the disorder is stress-related, but research does not clearly support this interpretation. When physical relaxation is effective in promoting sleep, it is understood to be the racing thoughts that are actually being treated. The relaxation procedure serves only to distract the person from compulsive thinking (Brokovec, 1982). The person apparently finds it difficult to concentrate upon worrying thoughts whilst simultaneously relaxing the kneecaps, the eyebrows, and the navel. With luck, sleep may intrude before the relaxation procedure is completed.

Accepting this interpretation, that the benefits of relaxation primarily might be to distract the person's thoughts, it might be more sensible to apply therapeutic interventions which are more directly aimed at the disturbing thinking patterns. This point was borne out in a Stanford University study which employed a combination of approaches: a relaxation tape for use at home, and instruction in daytime stress reduction. Of these techniques, it was found that psychological therapy aimed at active daytime stress reduction was the most effective method of reducing sleep onset insomnia (Fuerst, 1983). Again, in an article somewhat misleadingly headed 'Home use of recorded relaxation execises as initial treatment for stress related disorder', (Sherman, 1982) patients who were diagnosed as 'uncomplicated chronic anxiety neurosis' were given a 12 minute 'progressive muscle relaxation' tape to be used each day for one month. This study reported no significant change in anxiety at one month, or at six months. Spielberger's State and Trait Anxiety Scale was used to measure stress (Sherman, 1982). This somewhat cautionary summary about the benefits of relaxation does not mean that the technique is of no value in stress management, but simply means that more active therapies should be used as well.

As indicated above, hypnosis techniques are often referred to at the same time as relaxation 'therapy'. Hypnosis can indeed induce a feeling of physical relaxation. Further than this, the hypnosis procedure can be used to implant suggestions for alternative evaluations and alternative reactions to life. This does not mean the glossy-journal style of 'positive thinking'. Positive thinking is doomed to failure. Life is not full of events that can be evaluated as positive experiences and it is the experience of most clinicians that the disappointment which patients experience after the false hope of jingoistic 'positive thinking therapy' is worse than the 'pretherapy' state. However, the use of rational responses, less negative and more realistic thoughts can be practised under hypnosis with valuable advances in mood control being achieved. This use of hypnosis as an adjunct to active therapy is reviewed below.

In summary, relaxation alone, whether or not it is linked with hypnosis, will often fail to provide relief from stress and stress-related problems. This is particularly evident when a patient is operating under severe external pressures. Even if a relaxing trance state were to be achieved in the clinic, as soon as the pateint returns to normal consciousness and perceives that overwhelming forces are still present, the stress-related thinking patterns will return. This is the situation in instances of severe work-related pressures, financial crisis, or personal tragedy. For some of these, the patient will simply not be able to imagine a situation where a response other than serious stress can result. Efforts to intervene in the external factors may therefore be indicated. The approaches which can change the balance of external factors include Family Therapy, time management training, and advice from legal parties or social workers.

2. Talking therapies

When dealing with seriously anxious patients it is important to bear in mind that stress interferes with a person's ability to concentrate. There will be lapses of concentration, and these lapses will occur each minute. It is therefore vital that the talking procedure should not overtax the patient's present abilities. Long sessions of therapy will be wasted because the patient simply cannot follow, process, and remember the application of what is being said or discussed. The patient will, however, be aware of this inability to concentrate, and recognition of this problem may add to the patient's distress.

Intensive psychotherapy has been shown to produce long-term neuroses in soldiers suffering from battle stress, whereas short-term, directive interventions followed by a rapid return to normal duties leads to very few long-term problems (Abraham, 1982). It is not yet known whether or not these results translate to civilian problems, but the warning is there. Despite this warning, evidence which indicates the need for immediate short-term therapy combined with a rapid return to duties is ignored by employees, unions, and the legal professional when dealing with cases of worker stress, for example, with ambulance officers, police, and teachers. The growing frequency of long-term problems in these professions, often relabelled as 'burnout', provides ample evidence that a 'new' approach based upon established stress management procedures is required.

Simple, direct and systematic refutation of irrational beliefs can often help, and this is the approach of Rational Emotive Therapy (RET). Clear, single-sentence challenges to the patient's irrational beliefs are made. These challenges include simple questions such as:

Where is the proof?
How do you know?
Why must you?
Why is that an untrue statement?
How would that be so terrible?
As long as you believe that, how will you feel?

(Walen *et al.*, 1980)

The verbal disputation may be accompanied by realistic and achievable positive imagery. If a particular place or situation is involved with the stress—

perhaps work for a school teacher, or a feared situation for a phobic patient—then therapy should include a plan for an early return to that place so that the stressful stimulii can be encountered and the new thought-management techniques applied in practice.

'Stress Inoculation' provides an approach to stress management which concentrates more on the use of positive imagery and the habit of positive self-talk as a means of blocking the destructive focus upon sress-producing beliefs. Underlying the development of the Stress Inoculation procedure was the proposition that a moderate amount of anxiety can be caused when a person imagines him or herself in a stressful situation. With suitable training this level of anxiety can be reduced. Regular experience with this reduced level of anticipatory stress, combined with mental rehearsing of positive self-statements and the imagination of positive outcomes, can enable a person to better cope with real-life stressors. Examples of positive self-statements (Ramm et al., 1981) are:

I can cope with these failings.
I'm not doing so bad really.
I am going to stay here come what may.

The stress inoculation approach has been successful with 'normal' people including volunteers from the community (e.g. Girodo et al., 1978), or students. This makes it of interest to people in business or those who are running the popular and often lucrative 'stress management courses'. In more serious clinical problems, the authors have successfully used an approximation of this procedure, combined with hypnosis, in the management of phobias.

Although Stress Inoculation is not necessarily used in conjunction with hypnosis, and therefore correctly comes under the heading of talking therapies rather than hypnosis, it is a procedure that can easily be adapted to hypnotic augmentation. In practice this overlap between procedures drawn from nominally different therapies is common since the target problem is the same; the problem of stress.

The use of positive imagery, where the clients imagine themselves to be in a problematic situation but imagine different feelings and thoughts, is also used in RET. The practitioners of RET also approve of the combination of this positive imagery with hypnosis (Walen et al., 1980). One particular case of combined therapy—hypnosis plus RET based cognitive restructuring—was reported to provide superior results in the treatment of test anxiety, guilt, anxiety neurosis, and migraine (Howard et al., 1982). This application of hypnosis enabled the therapist to direct the focus of the client's attention to any element of the sequence of events, thoughts, and behaviours which are involved in the unwanted outcome. A successful case dealing with the difficult problem of migraine was documented (Howard *et al.*, 1982) to illustrate the combination procedure. An outline of this case is presented here.

The client was a 30-year-old female who suffered severe migraine attacks almost daily. The headaches had begun when she was 12 years old. Psychological testing indicated that her response to stress-provoking events was repression, and conversion of the psychological tension into somatic symptoms.

The relative ineffectiveness of hypnosis as a single therapy first demonstrated over four weekly sessions of therapy. The standard tension-reducing suggestions were made, particularly those relating to relaxation of the head and shoulder regions. There was a minimal improvement in the number of reported migraines.

Over the following five months of hypnosis-augmented RET, steady reductions in migraine frequency were noted, until 'during the last 5 weeks of...[therapy]...migraine headaches were almost non-existent' (Howard *et al.*, 1982, p. 265). In addition to this, the patient's personality style (measured by Minnesota Multiphasic Personality Inventory scales changed from the formerly repressive type to a 'less defensive...[and]...emotionally more relaxed...'profile (Howard *et al.*, 1982, p. 266).

It was concluded that, although physiological changes such as vasodilation and abnormal distribution of cerebral blood supply are believed to be the final cause of the intense pain in migraine attacks, approaches to control these symptoms through biofeedback or relaxation/hypnosis may often fail if clinicians are unaware of the underlying psychological disorders. Failure to restructure faulty belief systems, combined with a concentration of the final physical symptom itself, might reinforce the patient's acceptance of the psychosomatic problem as a purely physical disorder.

3. Exercise

Physical work or exercise is often presented as a panacea for all mental ailments, and many physical ones too. Almost all studies on the effects of exercise report an improvement in mood state (e.g., Morgan and Horstman, 1976; Morgan *et al.*, 1970; Leddwidge, 1980). The most frequently reported improvements are a reduction in anxiety, tension, and depression. The improvements have been reported immediately after exercise (Markoff *et al.*, 1982) or after a regular exercise program has been followed (Ransford, 1982).

The apparent benefit of exercise is not just a phenomenon restricted to carefully controlled psychological experiments—in real life the advantages of exercise have been reported as well. Military bomb disposal work is acknowledged as a very high stress occupation. In this occupation it has been found that the most competent and least stressed bomb disposal experts were the most physically fit (Rachman, 1982). In another real life study, soldiers in the stressful situation of awaiting an enemy attack in Vietnam were evaluated for physiological manifestations of stress. The group who showed the lower chemical indices of stress (elevated levels of 17-hydroxycorticosteroids in urine) were those who were engaged in physical activities such as digging bunkers and erecting defences (Bourne, 1969). Notwithstanding the unreliability of chemical measures of stress outlined in Chapter 3, this report may be interpreted to indicate that physical exercise, or hard work, may help to relieve stress.

The mechanism whereby exercise works is at present unknown. There have been many theories, and there is generally a little evidence to support each one. The theories include:

1. An endorphin effect, now disputed (Chapter 3).
2. A supposition that exercise acts as a distraction or 'displacement activity' so that the person's mind is occupied with an alternative activity to the stress-related thoughts.
3. A view that exercise helps to prevent sleep disturbance, and, as well as being one of the symptoms of stress, sleep disturbance also helps to cause and maintain stress.
4. A rationalization that exercise raises some of the chemical correlates of stress, and so the person somehow gets used to the physiological consequences of being stressed.
5. A view that exercise represents a risk or challenge, and this helps to overcome thoughts about being worthless or inadequate.
6. A supposition that exercise usually occurs in a social context, and the increased social contact itself is therapeutic.

Each of these explanations has some empirical support - perhaps they all combine to produce the beneficial effect of exercise. If this is true then the composite effect of all these forces is terribly disappointing. Exercise has only a relatively weak therapeutic effect and it is especially weak in the light of the dramatic side effects it induces. No drug which caused such distressing physical changes (sweating, panting, racing heart, etc.) would be tolerated by the public, nor permitted by medical authorities. Furthermore, exercise has some distinctly negative effects. The case of elevated anxiety in exercise-intolerant patients was mentioned earlier (Chapter 3). Exercise is also apparently addictive and this can bring problems. Consistent runners who are unable to run for two or more weeks due to an injury become significantly more depressed, anxious, tense and confused than a group of runners who continued to exercise (Chan, 1981).

Overall, many of the beneficial effects of exercise have been attributed to the physical or physiological changes which exercise brings on. But we have emphasized the view that psychological factors create stress. The main psychological components of the stress equation were introduced at the beginning of this chapter. If exercise can directly reduce stress, then it should be possible to interpret this effect in the context of these psychological causes of stress. Taking the psychoanalytical formulation first, regular involvement in exercise could strengthen any, or all three, of the narcissistic beliefs. The consistent activity of facing a challenge and surviving - even excelling in some cases - could add support to the notion of invulnerability. Often physical activity is performed in a shared social setting, and this involvement with an additional group of peers who share certain goals and face similar difficulties can lead to improved belief in the idea of group support. Finally, if a leader, coach, or trainer is involved, this person could fill the role of the respected leader (the omnipotent servant).

From the Rational Emotive Therapy point of view, there appears to be little in an exercise program that will add to a person's ability to dispute irrational stress-producing beliefs. It is true that exercise may offer a chance for 'time out' from agonizing over unproductive interpretations of life, but, as we observed when discussing the value of relaxation as a sole therapy, a short respite from worrying does little to relieve chronic stress. The worries can, and do, return.

In summary it is probably true that exercise influences stress, but at present it is not possible to say whether it will increase or decrease stress in a particular patient, nor how exercise should be introduced in order to maximize the elusive beneficial effects. It is difficult to see how exercise alone could alter a person's habitual style of evaluating life events as stressful, or how it could prevent a person from suffering from the emotional consequences of irrational beliefs. It therefore seems most likely that if exercise is to be used in stress management program for a serious case of stress, then adjunctive psychotherapeutic approaches should be included.

4. Chemotherapy

There is certainly a need for a discussion of chemotherapy in a book on stress, but what can be said with confidence? There is growing disaffection for chemotherapy among clinicians and patients alike. We have not yet established the proper place for chemotherapy in the management of milder forms of psychological disturbance. There is simply too much money and too many vested interests involved in this contentious area to allow even-handed conclusions to be drawn. Some facts, however, are undisputed.

First, the drugs used in the treatment of stress do indeed reduce the symptoms of acute anxiety and therefore they help the patient to feel better. The drugs prescribed as anxiolytics are generally benzodiazepine derivatives. They are particularly useful in relieving acute anxiety brought about by specified threatening events. An example of this use has been reported in the management of anxiety prior to dental surgery (O'Boyle *et al.*, 1986). The patients had been previously separated into High Anxiety and Low Anxiety groups according to their reported fears of dental situations. In the experimental situation, the level of the pateints' stress was measured using Spielberger's State Anxiety Scale (reviewed in Chapter 4). The 'high anxious' group benefited significantly from the administration of benzodiazepine orally, 30 minutes prior to the operation. Their stress scores were reduced to near normal levels by the drug. This reduction in stress did not occur in a group of high anxiety pateints who were given placebo medication. The drug was reported to be of no benefit to the 'low anxious' groups, but this result was inevitable since they already had scores approaching the minimum possible on Spielberger's State Anxiety Scale.

Second, millions of people in the western world are on long term (several years) programs of drug usage. This continued use of anxiolytics is reinforced by the initial benefit that the patients can receive from their first experience with chemotherapy. In the example above, the patients who were helped to face their dental operation more calmly could, for example, decide that these drugs would be valuable in all threatening or worrying situations. Unfortunately, many practitioners have supported this method of handling life's demands.

There are people who tend to experience an excessive stress reaction to any threatening event, and many of them have been told to 'take a tablet at the slightest feeling of unease'. The patients do exactly this. The long term results of this medication regime are unfortunately not very good. The patient may suffer less acute anxiety, but at the same time he or she runs the grave risk of becoming psychologically addicted to the medication. They begin to believe that they cannot cope with life without medication. Without psychological intervention, this belief remains. They may also suffer physical withdrawal symptoms if the drug regime is terminated. In 1986, the first legal repercussions of this approach to patient management occurred. A woman was awarded substantial damages against a psychiatrist who had prescribed an anxiolytic for the treatment of 'stress symptoms'. After four years of continual medication she developed insomnia and began to hallucinate when she was taken off her medication. The possibility of legal action must be considered by all practitioners who treat an ongoing stress problem with drugs.

Third, in the pharmaceutical control of anxiety the presenting problem is often confused with a number of other distinct but related problems including depression and sleep disturbance. The first step in prescribing antianxiety drugs must be to ensure that the main problem is indeed anxiety, or stress. Stress is present in every patient who is suffering from depression, but the pharmacological treatment of this stress will not be successful, nor will it relieve the depression. The problem of incorrect diagnosis in cases of depression is not new: 'At every psychiatric out-patient clinic there are depressed patients who have been treated for months, even years by their general practitioner with anti-anxiety drugs. . .' (Davies, 1973, p. 20).

The continuing difficulty that general practitioners have in recognizing the difference between anxiety and depression was reconfirmed in a more recent study which dealt with referrals from general practitioners to psychologists. When the patient was referred to a psychologist for problems such as anxiety, phobias, psychosexual problems, or marital problems, up to 80% of the psychologists' diagnoses were in accord with the opinion of the referring doctor. However, with depressed patients, in only 13% of the cases had the doctor correctly diagnosed the disorder (Reid and Khan, 1983).

This problem of diagnosis is being overcome as more family physicians recognize the value of working collaboratively with a clinical psychologist. The psychologist is especially equipped to conduct an objective differential diagnosis of neurotic disorders, and is able to provide the necessary therapeutic interventions. At the same time, close cooperation with the family physician, who can manage the use of drugs where necessary, ensures that the patient does not lose contact with a usual source of aid and support—the general practitioner. The implementation of a cooperative regime between physician and psychologist avoids the concern that a management procedure based primarily upon the prescription of drugs 'should not replace the more important doctor involvement with the patient and his problems' (Davies, 1973, p. 20).

The conclusion that must be drawn from practical experience is that although antianxiety drugs are available, the need for confident diagnosis demands collaboration between the medical profession and the psychologist. This collaboration can then lead to a joint decision about the use of drugs alone, the use of an appropriate form of psychotherapy alone, or the combination of both treatments by both practitioners.

In summary, and with certainty, we can say that drugs do work in reducing the experience of stress, but perhaps not as well in the long term as prescribing habits would indicate. The use of drugs alone may be justified when a patient is facing a single, specific threatening event such as dental surgery. However, the administration of drugs does not change the patient's habitual processes for evaluating life events in a negative way—this treatment cannot therefore change the patient's general tendency to experience stress.

5. Diet and stress

Related to the idea that stress can be controlled by medication is the viewpont that everything we swallow could have an effect on stress levels. The clinician will be confronted with patients who have particular ideas about food and mood—and occasionally these ideas need to be challenged. Parents seem to be particularly vulnerable to stories about food and their children's problems, and in this way the interaction of food and psychology becomes central to stress management.

Taking into account all the evidence, it is certain that food can lead to stress. The only question is: does it cause stress to the person eating the food, or does stress only come from thinking about food? Perhaps this question cannot be answered at the moment, but some of the evidence relating to it can be presented. Some of the studies described below do not directly relate to stress, but to other manifestations of psychological discomfort, including expressions of anger, or difficulty in concentration. It was indicated in Chapter 4 that these problems can be correlates of stress. Although in some cases the experimental links are tenuous, the studies presented below accumulate some of the evidence that diet can directly influence the experience of stress.

A clear connection between food and mood is evident when people abstain from eating at all. The effects of not eating are nearly all bad. Eating no food causes people to suffer from fatigue, depression, anxiety, impaired judgement, and, in extreme cases, death. Some of these effects can easily be tested. A more contentious issue is the idea that certain foods actually cause people to develop psychological disturbances, including stress.

The 'junk food' industry is often singled out as being behind many of society's ills, including psychological disturbances. A series of studies supporting the psychopathological consequences of junk food have been described by Schoenthalar (e.g., Schoenthalar, 1983). His subjects were adolescents who were in custody after having been apprehended for various crimes. In one report, which covered a two year period, dietary revisions involved the replacement of soft drinks (sodas) and 'junk' food with fruit juices and 'nutritious snacks'. There was a reported decrease in 'antisocial behaviour' among the inmates while they were on the nutritious diet. An interesting aspect of this study is that it was described as a 'double blind' study, which means that neither the experimenter nor the subjects knows who is on the special diet, and who is on the standard diet. But it is clear that this criterion was not fulfilled, and so the enthusiasm of the researcher has coloured his reporting of the experiment, at least a little. One wonders whether the marvellous results might also have been coloured by the enthusiasm of the experimenter.

Another study which demonstrated the bad effects of junk food involved children at an elementary school. It was proposed that children's behaviour and learning processes would be badly influenced by the ingestion of junk food. Children were therefore given a modified diet where refined carbohydrate foods were eliminated and fresh fruits and juices, whole wheat flour, honey, and unprocessed foods were substituted for other foods. The teachers reported that, after a period of six months on this diet, significant improvements were achieved in both behaviour and learning patterns of the children (Warden *et al.*, 1982). A corresponding association between food and 'stress symptoms' was also found in university students (Bagley, 1981). In this study the consumption of 'non-nutritious' food was significantly related to behavioural problems and physical and emotional complaints.

An interesting and different contribution to the food-mood story was brought out by a questionnaire survey that asked which foods a person would prefer to eat when he or she was experiencing certain moods. In general, people tended to choose from 'healthy' nonprocessed foods when they felt friendly, relaxed and self-confident. They indicated that a preference for junk foods would accompany feelings of boredom, anxiety, guilt or frustration. In this survey, meat was most often preferred in association with the positive emotions, and specifically seemed to be associated with 'being in love' (Lyman 1982.) It is not possible to accord great predictive power to results which are based on the question 'what would you prefer to eat if you felt...'. But this study could be taken to indicate that fast foods, in themslves, are not the cause of bad moods. Perhaps the apparent association is a result of a subtle interaction between mood, social factors, and the effort involved in making a meal.

There have been other similar studies claiming to show the psychological benefits of changed food regimes, and from these studies it would appear that modern preprocessed food causes stress and other psychological problems. However, some carefully conducted experiments, combined with more even-handed reviews of the literature have not supported this proposal (Trites and Tryphonas, 1983; Waksman 1983). It is certainly true that a diet which is devoid of essential elements, one that is nutritionally unbalanced, can lead to physical ill health. It is quite orthodox to assume that a susceptibility to physical malaise should be accompanied by a decrease in psychological robustness, an attenuation of coping skills, and an elevation of levels of stress. But the junk food studies go further than this simple suggestion that physical illness leads to mental distress. The studies appear to suggest that, for a variety of reasons, processed food leads to stress and related disorders. For example although they are nutritionally similar, honey does not cause stress while refined white sugar does. At present, some of the supportive studies lack rigor and appropriate control groups. Yet there is enough apparent evidence to support belief in a relationship between food and mood. However, strong claims about this relationship await solid research findings. A clinician who is interested in the total package of attitudes and habits which lead to stress must consider dietary advice as a legitimate component in his or her approach to therapy, but it is possible to overstate the expected effects of a 'nutritious and natural' diet. It has yet to be shown that a diet consisting of brown rice and lettuce leaves will provide immunity against the experience of stress (or, indeed, against many other health risks or diseases).

D. EXAMPLES OF CLINICAL MANAGEMENT

Clinical mangement of anxiety conditions is an ongoing problem. There is no single best approach, but a specialist in the area can generally select from a range of approaches to find a means of giving some help to the stressed individual. The absence of a single successful procedure has been noted as a continuing problem: 'The frequency of free-floating eanxiety makes it an important problem, but its treatment is still problematic. A powerful, reliable and lasting form of management remains to be developed for chronic anxiety states' (Ramm *et al.*, 1981).

This recognized deficiency has not prevented zealots from claiming that their particular approach, or potion, is universally effective. But we should regard such claims as either miraculous or else exaggerated. This somewhat negative summary does not mean that stress cannot be treated, it simply means that each case must be interpreted on its own merits. It also means that a therapist who is trained in just one modality cannot expect to successfully manage a majority of the stress problems with which patients will present. Each of the therapeutic approaches outlined above has its place of application, and the intending stress counsellor should attend courses and study appropriate texts to learn more of the techniques of each approach. There are, however, some cases which cannot easily be matched with a particular type of therapy. The following clinical cases will provide examples treatment programs which have been effective in certain unusual cases.

1. Case 1—Hyperhydrosis: a psychosomatic symptom of stress

The idea that the mind is involved in the manifestation of obviously physical symptoms is an idea which has received attention and also criticism throughout this century. Modern clinicians accept the principle that psychological factors are involved in many physical diseases. More particuarly they accept that the onset of stress, or exposure to stressful demands, can be a powerful cause of disorders. The unfortunate consequence of this realization is that, when practitioners accept that patients should receive physical symptomatic treatment *as well as* concurrent psychological therapy, the practitioner often perceives him or herself as not only a family doctor (or an allergy specialist) but suddenly becomes a stress consultant as well (at least in the practitioner's own eyes). With a few glances at a glib paperback book on stress control, the medical practitioner advises his or her patients that now the whole person, mind and body, will be treated.

The recognition that mind and body both need to be treated does not equip a physician to become a therapist. The broadest possible background of psychological (psychiatric) training is necessary to deal with the complications of psychosomatic disease. This proposition is not new: 'There are no exclusive relationships between personality...and the site of disturbance of somatic function' (Collison, 1980, p. 328, summarizing Wolfe, 1947). There is no single psychopathological cause of psychosomatic disorders, and there is therefore no simple do-it-yourself approach that can make a person into a stress consultant. This warning about the need for appropriate training in stress management is of course general, but it is perhaps most important in the management of psychosomatic disorders. The following case should be regarded more as an article of interest, rather than a recipe for treating similar (or dissimilar) problems.

The case selected refers to the treatment of a woman with hyperhydrosis. Hyperhydrosis is characterized by excessive sweating of the palms and the axillae. The problem was almost always related to the stress of social situations. The patient did not report any problem of excessive sweating when at home relaxing, but the problem arose when any form of threat or demand was present—and this could have been the simple occasion of having a drink with friends at the local bar. Parties and job interviews were accompanied by a flood of unwanted perspiration which literally poured from the affected area and dripped on the floor, contaminated other people, or spoiled important pieces of paper. Even if the cause of the problem was not stress, it is easy to see that stress was always the result of such an attack.

The symptoms of a disorder like this are usually resistant to conservative treatments such as the local application of normal antiperspirants and, although some topical applications are effective, surgical intervention is often required (Savin, 1983). Lerer and Jacobwitz (1981) have discussed hyperhydrosis from a psychological point of view. They considered the possibility of interacting personality variables, and perceived the need for long-term psychotherapy, but little prospect of rapid relief was offered. Robertshaw (1979) has discussed the physiological mechanisms which regulate the sweating response, but was unable to provide an obvious mechanism for therapy.

The typical patient does not present with any other form of related organic disorder. The symptoms seem simply to be associated with particular situations. This observation places the precipitating factors within the psychological domain. The linking of the problem response with a range of stimulus situations can be understood as a learned psychophysiological response. This understanding leads to the expectation of a psychological method for controlling the problem. In support of this expectation there has been some success reported for biofeedback; however, it was suggested that a more specific form of psychological treatment could prove more useful (Duller and Gentry, 1980). Following on from the proposal that a psychological treatment should be developed, the authors (King and Stanley, 1986) undertook the study of a single case of hyperhydrosis.

The patient was a female, Barbara, who was aged 28 years. She was living in a stable relationship with a male partner and was employed in a clerical position. She reported being satisifed with her general situation in life. Clinical evaluation indicated that she was non-neurotic. Testing with the Minnesota Multiphasic Personality Inventory revealed no significant scoring pattern on any of the scales. She was referred by a surgeon for treatment of her 'anxiety', a problem which the referring doctor believed was due to her excessive sweating.

Barbara's history indicated that she suffered from profuse sweating from the armpits in all social occasions, but obtained relief from this when at home with her male partner. She had undergone surgery to remove most of the active sweat glands, but this had not prevented the sweating problem. She had previously been to relaxation classes, but these also had no effect. Barbara openly expressed doubt that psychological treatment could have any effect on her problem due to her very unsatisfactory history of treatment.

a. Formulation of a therapeutic approach

As indicated above, an important part of the treatment of any stress-related problem is the need to combine the particular issues and the general class of problem into a formulation that should be expected to work. Although placebo effects are rewarding for both practitioner and patient, when they work, in order to learn from the case in hand it is worth while trying to understand what effects placebo mechanisms will have in the therapeutic approach. A cautionary note is sounded here because in all psychological interventions success may be due to no more than a placebo effect, and to rely upon this effect is really no better than employing black magic. In the present case, surgery could be regarded as a valid form of placebo therapy. It had good face validity; it could have even worked. But it was unsuccessful. Given this demonstrated resistance to placebo therapy, any gains due to the planned psychological intervention could be reasonably interpreted as being specific to the proposed therapy.

As indicated earlier in this book the emotional response to stress is accompanied by some changes in body chemistry (that is, physiological changes). In particular, the adrenal system and the hormone levels it controls are most commonly the focus of stress-related changes. Adrenal activity is also indicated in the sweating response, particularly under circumstances when thermal homeostasis does not require it (Robertshaw, 1979). But it would be premature to say that hyperhydrosis is an indication that a malfunction in the adrenal system is the cause of the problem. The problem is that sweating had become an automatic response to social situations, whether or not this response included the elevation of circulating catecholamines, or stimulation of the sympathetic nervous system.

It has long been recognized that the pairing of an automatic (autonomic) response can occur with a particular stimulus. This is the basis for the classical conditioning pioneered by Pavlov, using dogs. Such a response can also occur in humans. In the present case, the response of sweating—however it was learned—had now been generalized across a wide range of situations. This could be taken as evidence that this particular subject was quite susceptible to the processes of classical conditioning. The treatment devised therefore aimed at a manipulation of Barbara's susceptibility to conditioning using a program of hypnosis-based mental imagery.

Normal sweating in humans does not occur below a skin temperature of 34°C (McCaffrey et al., 1979; Winslow et al., 1973). Slightly altered thresholds can occur for thermoregulatory sweating. For instance values as low as 32.6°C have been reported for patients suffering from anorexia nervosa (Luck and Wakeling, 1980). The control of skin temperature to maintain a relatively stable value of skin temperature is at least as complex as the control of sweating. It is best regarded as an automatic adjustment which is under the control of a variety of mechanisms. Sudden changes in the environment can interfere with normal stability; for example, immersion in cold water can produce local vasoconstriction and a rapid reduction of skin temperatures.

The treatment program devised for Barbara used these effects. It was intended to give her some voluntary means of controlling the unwanted, classically conditioned response of sweating. She was to be given a new conditioned response which was the inability to sweat. This is associated with reduced skin temperature. The new conditioned stimulus was the repetition of the word 'cold'.

The first stage of the treatment was the acquisition of the conditioned response. Barbara was asked to take cold showers daily for two weeks, particularly making sure that the cold water ran over the parts of her body which exhibited excessive sweating; that is, her armpits. Whilst taking the shower she was asked to repeat the word 'cold' out loud, and to take notice of any side effects of the treatment such as cold shivers. These additional signs would be valuable in adding realism to the hypnosis phase to come.

After the showering phase, Barbara underwent hypnosis. After the trance induction she was instructed to imagine herself in a target social situation where there was a mild threat. A situation where she was with two or three friends at a hotel was selected. At this stage of the trance it was suggested that she think the trigger word 'cold'. Further suggestions relating to her experiences in the cold shower, the cold shivers, for example, were made. A tape recording of this session was made and Barbara listened to the tape daily for the next week. In addition, a suggestion was made during the hypnotic trance that she should be able to daydream the important aspects of the tape session at any time of the day.

After a week of this practice a real life situation was confronted. With a successful result, new target situations were inserted into the taped program. After one more week an opportunity to test the program in a major target situation arose; a large party. Barbara reported no incidence of sweating during this evening. She then indicated that she was satisfied with her progress and therapy was terminated after a total of five weeks. She reported that she no longer had a stress problem in social situations.

In summary, this case illustrated the treatment of a real physical problem, excessive sweating, which was certainly associated with stress. Now an important aspect of the experience of stress is the amount of self-doubt and negative thoughts under which we suffer. In this case there were many self-condemnatory thoughts involved, relating to the socially unacceptable level of her sweating. It could reasonably be argued that a cognitive approach to the problem, aimed at reducing the anxiety she felt about the problem, would have been successful as well. But in this case the therapist chose to formulate a direct assault upon the physical symptoms. The result was that a very resistant symptom was controlled, and the patient's reported levels of stress were dramatically reduced.

2. Case 2—Repetitive strain injury, phobia and stress

This case involved the psychological treatment of a young woman who was suffering from a combination of psychological symptoms which included stress, increasing outbursts of anger and fear of thunder, and which was developing into a full-scale phobia. In addition to these problems she had tenosynovitis in the hands, apparently associated with keyboard work at her place of employment. She was referred for psychological help for her 'nervous' problems. The formulation of a management strategy in this case demands a good working knowledge of the nature of the physical disorder; that is, painful tendons in the hands.

Tenosynovitis, or painfully inflamed tendons, can occur in any part of the body due to some type of abusive overload. In the 1980s the occurrence of this problem in the hands of keyboard operators reached the proportions of an epidemic. Different names have been given to the disorder, among them Repetitive Strain Injury (RSI). RSI was first diagnosed in the hands but there are now cases where RSI has been recognized in the arms and shoulders. Other areas of the body will no doubt fall victim to this disease as well. RSI has become a major issue in workers' compensation cases. For people who are employed in the public sector, particularly, RSI has emerged as a major reason for sick leave. Medical practitioners seem unable to treat RSI successfully. Apparently there are some factors in addition to physical overload which are associated with the disorder.

The additional factors which are involved in the RSI epidemic are psychological, and more than this, they have been identified as being linked with stress (Linehan, 1985). Serious studies of the whole problem have concluded that general stress, caused either within the work environment or from outside the workplace, can play a role in the development of the symptoms (McPhee 1980, 1983). At least one part of the mechanism linking stress with tendon problems could involve circulating uric acid levels (Smart *et al.*, 1980). An earlier chapter indicated that uric acid levels are elevated in response to stress, particularly during the anticipatory phase of the evaluation procedure. When uric acid levels become elevated, the acid crystals may precipitate in musculoskeletal connective tissue. Where there is tendon damage, some of the chemical changes associated with the inflammatory process specifically attract the deposition of the uric acid crystals. These crystals tend to increase the inflammatory processes and enhance further deposition. A self-enhancing cycle is thus produced at the tissue level, while, at the psychological level, the increased discomfort, the reduced self-efficacy, and the general scepticism from colleagues relating to RSI, all combine to produce the mood-related changes which lead to high levels of uric acid. Like the inflammatory process, the mood disorder, involving stress and the anticipation of further negative outcomes, becomes a self-sustaining cycle.

Overall, it is the combination of physical overload, work-related stressors, and individual differences in the tendency to experience stress, which seem to put an individual at risk. When a person becomes aware of the initial vague symptoms of RSI, the widespread hysteria that has been generated about this disorder can precipitate a serious escalation of the psychological stress, and inevitably a worsening of the physical symptoms.

While the presenting symptoms of RSI are apparently physical, it has never been seriously disputed that psychological factors play an important part in the development of the problem, and also in the affected person's adjustment to the condition. The major symptom in RSI is swelling of the tendons with associated persistent pain caused by finger movements. In the broader use of the term RSI to cover any (work-related) tendon problems, the pain comes from movement of the associated limb. The experience of pain, and the reaction of a person to this experience, has both a physical and a psychological component (Elton *et al.*, 1983). Therefore, with RSI we have a problem which is believed to include significant psychological factors in its development, and psychological factors also are involved in the management of its chief symptom, pain. Stress is perhaps the most important of these 'psychological factors' which are associated with RSI.

Given the importance of stress in the development and treatment of RSI, there is an obvious need for a psychological component to be included in the treatment program for an RSI victim. This need for psychological therapy is even more important when the management of a pain condition is complicated by employment-related compensation issues (Elton and Stanley, 1982). However, the recognition of the psychological component in the problem has not led to appropriate action in the clinical setting. Current treatment of the problem generally involves an immediate recommendation of withdrawal from all keyboard work, and, in many cases, the treatment includes a complete rest from the work situation altogether. This is often combined with complete immobilization of the affected area, and no recourse to stress management procedures. Not only is this inappropriate from the psychological point of view, it also happens to be a bad way to manage the physical symptoms. The problem does not get better, and the consequences are continued pain and increased stress. To elaborate on the interaction between bad physical therapy and no psychological help it is useful to review what is known about the physical side of the disorder.

Given the emotional and economic connotations of RSI, it is better to discuss the physical aspects of an analogous injury, but one which is devoid of an emotional overlay. Such a complaint is found in Achilles tendonitis.

Unlike RSI, Achilles tendon injuries typically occur outside the work place and are unlikely to attract financial rewards. Achilles tendon problems usually occur during the recreational pursuits such as jogging. Achilles tendon problems are like RSI in several ways:

a. The patient complains of pain when the affected part is moved, and although the pain might diminish during a period of use, it is subsequently worse after a short rest period.
b. The injury is exacerbated by neglect of the problem and also by continued use.
c. Achilles tendon problems do not respond immediately to unimodal therapies such as ultrasound.
d. In cases of severe clinical mismanagement or neglect surgical interventions appear to be the only appropriate method of treatment.

A final similarity between Achilles tendon problems and RSI is that many medical practitioners and physiotherapists seem to be unaware of the apropriate treatment regime. Worse than this, they often employ treatment programs which are simply wrong.

In the case of Achilles tendon problems, the consequence of wrong treatment is little more than inconvenience, albeit it is sometimes a serious one. The level of inconvenience can extend from an unnecessarily long period where the athlete's sport cannot be pursued, to the possibility of long-term disability. In the case of RSI, incorrect treatment leads to excessive compensation awards with an ultimate effect on the economies of insurance; it also leads to long-term stress-related psychological problems with disrupting and negative consequences to career path and personal relationships.

An example of wrong treatment of tendon disorder is the local injection of steroids (cortisone) to relieve inflammation and pain. Consistent reports (e.g., Smart *et al.*, 1980) indicating that steroid treatment weakens the tendon and increases the prospect of subsequent total rupture have been ignored by practitioners treating Achilles tendon problems. The steroids do indeed relieve some of the symptoms and allow the affected individual to undertake increased activity, but at the same time they interfere with the healing process. The mechanism underlying this interference has been described:

> Tissue repair involves the ingrowth of fibrous connective tissue and blood vessels into the damaged region. Stimulated to invade the area by the inflammatory process, fibroblasts lay down collagen fibers, the foundation for connective tissue. Glucocorticoids (the principal anti-inflammatory steroids) impair the proliferation of fibroblasts, reducing their capacity to produce mature collagen. The formation of fibrin from fibrinogen, the aggregation of platelets, and capillary proliferation into the damaged tissue are all inhibited by glucocorticoids, delaying the healing process (Smart *et al.*, 1980, p. 236).

Apart from cortisone injections, the two other most common treatments for RSI are ultrasound physiotherapy and total immobilization. The ineffectiveness of ultrasound speaks for itself—patients occasionally get trivial levels of immediate relief from discomfort, but improvement simply does not follow. It has been suggested that in addition to being ineffective, ultrasound may disturb the tissue in the tendon, and 'potentiate an inflammatory rection' (Smart *et al.*, 1980). For the physiotherapist, ultrasound therapy offers a much less physically demanding approach compared with deep transverse massage. The latter approach produces some therapeutic benefits in cases of soft tissue injuries because it has an analgesic effect which has, as a major consequence, that the patient will not voluntarily immobilize the affected tissue by not using it. Scar tissue formation and adhesions are therefore reduced during the healing phase (de Bruijn, 1983). Immobilization should be avoided in cases of RSI and total immobiliation should never be selected as the treatment of choice. The consequences of this form of treatment are degeneration of both the affected and the undamaged tissue, a reduction in tendon vascularization, a reduced rate of healing, and seriously increased potentiation for further damage when the immobilization is discontinued.

An additional procedure which is popular in the treatment of almost every form of soft tissue sports injury is the use of ice, or 'cryotherapy'. A typical prescription might be to pack the affected tendon in ice for 15 minutes, twice a day. Despite its great popularity with the sports medicine fraternity, ice treatment is not normally selected for RSI victims, although the nature of the injuries is essentially identical. However, while it is not common, ice treatment will no doubt be used in some cases of RSI as the therapists perceive the parallel physical nature of sports and work injuries.

This difference in treatment is certainly indicative of a difference in therapists' perceptions and the issue deserves further investigation. For the moment, however, our discussion is limited to the appropriateness of ice treatment for RSI patients. Our aim is to help the RSI victim psychologically, and we are only considering the likely physical treatment regimes in order to see whether or not ineffective treatment is exacerbating the accompanying stress problems. In line with this aim, let us state simply that ice therapy for soft tissue injury appears to be based upon fundamental ignorance of human thermophysiological responses.

The aim of ice treatment is to reduce tissue temperature, and thus to reduce the pooling of fluids in the affected areas. In fact it is not really possible to reduce human tissue, even at the periphery like the fingers or toes, to 0°C, except in cases where an individual is lost in the snow and is dying of hypothermia. The paradoxical effect of placing tissue in an environment of approximately 0°C is actually to cause enhanced blood flow. This effect is called cold-induced vasodilation. It is the means by which the body prevents cold injury by excessive cooling of local areas.

For example, the temperature of the back of the hands will not drop permanently below about 15°C (Hellstrom et al., 1970; Wyndham and Wilson-Dickson, 1951), and efforts to produce temperatures lower than this will result in:

a. Great pain during the first few exposures.
b. A relatively rapid development of an anticipatory vasodilation response.
c. The redirection of body heat, and where necessary *the entire heat output* of the body (Newman and Breckenridge, 1968) to the ice-surrounded part in an effort to combat the unacceptable cooling effect.
d. Damage to cell tissue in the affected area (Lievens and Leduc, 1983).

The protective mechanism of increased blood flow at temperatures near 0°C has long been known, at least by those who are familiar with the physiology of the human body with which they are tampering. For example, Brown and Page (1952) demonstrated that there is greater blood flow when the hands are immersed in water at 5°C compared with immersion in water at 10°C or 20°C. Even more chilling than the application of direct ice packs is a bath of stirred ice water. It was found that one hand can maintain a heat loss of 70 W when it is exposed to stirred ice water, provided that the body is kept warm. This heat loss represents the entire heat output of a person at rest.

The appropriate way to use cryotherapy in the treatment of tendon injury is to use a medium which is about 12°C, that is cold water. A medium of this temperature brings with it all the benefits anticipated from the ice treatment regimen with neither excessive pain or tissue damage (Lievens and Leduc, 1983).

a. Management of repetitive strain injury

First it must be stated that repetitive strain injury does include real physical damage with real physical pain. If the physical treatment applied in cases of RSI includes selections from the above list, then the patient is probably receiving inappropriate therapy and inappropriate therapy does not make people better. It does not help their psychological mood either. Proper treatments for tendon injuries have been investigated and described (e.g. Smart *et al.*, 1980). The components of an appropriate program should include some or all of the following techniques.

i. Relative immobilization

Treatment of an inflamed soft tissue injury of any kind should first involve a withdrawal from all activities that enhance or induce the symptoms of tendonitis. This withdrawal is not the same as total immobilization (plaster cast or rigid bandage). The period of reduced activity should be for seven to 10 days after the patient first presents with painful tendons. It would be hoped that, as members of the workforce develop greater confidence in the ability of practitioners to successfully treat RSI, they will apply for treatment sooner rather than applying for compensation later.

ii. Stretching and exercise

The phase of relative inactivity should include regular stretching and gentle strengthening exercises. The result of a stretching and strengthening program is enhanced tendon vascularization, with its consequences of improved rate of tissue repair. The stretching also helps to overcome the problem of adhesion formation during the healing phase. A period of total inactivity produces quite the opposite effect and thus renders the tendon more liable to future injury. In the case of RSI, the stretching should be applied to the full range of movement of all arm and hand joints. The stretch should be held for between 10 and 20 seconds, relaxed, then repeated. Strengthening exercises should involve pushing against or lifting an appropriate load five to 10 times at first. Progressive increased resistance is recommended.

iii. Cryotherapy

As indicated above, ice packing has become a popular remedy for many soft tissue injuries. Although the acute application of ice to a new traumatic injury might be effective, the systematic use of ice is unnecessary and may be counterproductive. To take advantage of the benefits of cryotherapy, regular immersion of the affected area in ample cold water (between 10°C and 12°C) is recommended. It is important that the cool bath have constant replenishment to avoid the raising of bath temperature. This can be achieved by running a tap, at least in cold climates.

iv. Return to activity

A program of gradual return to the suspected causal activity should follow the relative inactivity period. This gradual return should be steady and systematic, with no sudden increase in workload. A satisfactory program would be:

day 1:	5 minutes of the activity
day 2:	no activity
day 3:	5 minutes of the activity
day 4:	no activity
day 5 and 7:	10 minutes of the activity
day 6 and 8:	no activity
day 9 and 11:	15 minutes of activity
day 13 and 15:	20 minutes of activity.

At the end of one month of this systematic increase in activity, the patient should be able to return to normal activity.

v. Psychological management

The present situation is that RSI occurs as a poorly understood and badly managed complaint which is generally associated with serious social, economic and psychological complications. An effective program must therefore include psychological assessment and psychological management at an early stage. The realistic situation is that the patient might not be referred for psychological help until serious psychopathological conditions have developed due to a combination of insensitive attitudes and frustration with an ineffective physical treatment program. Chronic pain from a condition which is not improving is itself a source of chronic anger—and the management of anger is a specialist problem in itself.

The following case history will illustrate how the complex interactive factors of an RSI case can be overcome with a combination of appropriate physical and psychological techniques.

'Judy' was referred for psychological help with the following note:

Dear Doctor,
Thankyou for seeing Judy who has several phobias, particularly thunder and lightning, and recently strong winds. She is also under considerable stress at work and is showing signs of depression, with multiple neurotic symptoms, poor sleeping and a tendency to close herself off from old friends.
    I hope you can help her.

Judy was 27 years old and married, but with no children. Her only past psychological/psychiatric encounter had been when she was 12; she had been to a psychiatrist 'on and off' for four years for 'nervous' problems. At the time of consultation she worked in the office section of a large supermarket chain. She reported that her present job was demoralizing; it involved looking at microfilm records. Her 'real job' involved keyboard duties but she was not able to do this work because of her RSI. She had suffered from RSI in the hands and wrists four times during the last two years. She had last been declared 'cured' from RSI in February. It was now July. Judy liked to play tennis and table tennis, but she could do neither now because of the RSI.

    This case has so many complicating features that it cannot be regarded as typical of any particular class of patient, but it clearly illustrates the need to consider the psychological profile of a person who contracts RSI. Notice that the referral did not include any mention of RSI, and the very real ways in which RSI was limiting her in activities that she preferred.

    The special aspect of Judy's case which had prompted the referral was a developing phobia about bad weather of all types, commencing with a (reported) long history of fear of thunder and lightening. She said that when she was young she used to sleep in the central passage of the family house during thunder storms. She reported that about two and a half years ago she had been nearly hit by lightning twice whilst in a car.

    Psychological problems appeared to be present long before the onset of the RSI, but the RSI was obviously adding to the burden of undermining beliefs that were producing what was now a clear case of chronic stress with a tendency to develop further serious psychopathology. The RSI could be seen to directly contradict the first narcissistic defence of invulnerability. With this gone, pre-existing fears about thunder and lightning were able to expand their influence on her. The monsters of the id were escaping.

    It was decided to suggest a new approach to the management of her RSI, based upon the above principles. She had already had more than the minimum period of relative inactivity as she had voluntarily withdrawn from almost any activity which used the hands. The work situation was complicated by compensation difficulties, but we had here the chance to work with her sporting interests. She had not touched her table tennis bat for about one month, the period of the present bout of RSI. She had believed that to do so would invite serious long term injury. The new program involved regular stretching exercises, firm self-massage of the sore tendons, and a return to 'exercise' commencing with five minutes of table tennis bat exercise each alternate day in a progression as described above.

As for Judy's phobic reaction to bad weather, it was believed that this could diminish as her confidence returned with the control of her RSI. However, Judy's second appointment involved a hypnotic trance induction and the pairing of a feeling of relaxation with heavy breathing. Essentially this employed the hyperventilaton technique described below in detail in the case of agoraphobia, but a process of systematic desensitization using mental imagery was employed rather than *in vivo* exposure. This mental imagery involved first practising the ability to capture a sense of feeling good, and then to replace negative reactions to thunder with these good feelings. The situation used to define feeling good was the pleasure she achieved from playing a really successful game of table tennis. This image was deliberately selected because of its power to reinforce the waning belief in personal invulnerability.

The third aspect of Judy's case was her deteriorating ability to handle social and work-related relationships. On the first session she was asked to fill out one Profile of Mood State form (see Chapter 4) each day for a week. The resulting profile was shown to her. It indicated regular peaks of anger, and she was able to see that this anger was indeed alienating her from her peers. In this, the third narcissistic defence (relating to group support) was also under attack. During the course of the next two months the major part of her therapy was devoted to developing the habit of rational thinking and the experience of rational emotions in response to situations at work. From this work she improved in her ability to handle perceived criticism, and developed a more stable sense of self confidence. As expected, this improvement in emotional control was paralleled by a dwindling of her need for further help in managing her phobic reactions.

By mid September Judy was able to play table tennis without pain or resulting tendonitis. On the few occasions that she tended to feel upset about bad weather she employed the lessons from the mental imagery program, leading to more successful (less traumatic) responses. By mid October she had returned to her original keyboard job with no difficulties.

b. Summary

RSI is often a physical manifestation of psychological problems. It is a physical disorder which in itself involves minimal injury and pain. However, when combined with psychological factors it can become crippling both physically and psychologically. Although in some cases a purely physical regimen may lead to improvement, a return of the symptoms might be expected if the underlying psychological pathology is not uncovered. The chance of success for a purely physical program is greatly reduced if the program is not based upon methods which work. Despite this inappropriate management techniques are regularly suggested. Psychological problems can only be expected to worsen if the real physical pain and disability from the RSI is not relieved.

The above case showed how the presentation of an interwoven pattern of RSI and psychological problems can be dealt with if *appropriate* physical and psychological modalities are combined.

3. Case 3—Hyperventilation, anxiety and agoraphobia

The problem of agoraphobia is a difficult one. It certainly includes the experience of a quite terrible emotional response of severe stress, but it seems to include a very special form of the stress response, the panic attack. Panic attacks were mentioned in the physiological section of this book (Chapter 3). The background and practical approach in the case study below shows how, even in the face of an uncertain cause, psychological management is possible.

In line with Freud's original proposals, anxiety is normally expected to occur in situations perceived as threatening or dangerous. In such situations, anxiety is an adaptive response and usually leads to action designed to reduce the level of threat. But anxiety becomes abnormal when it occurs without sufficient reason or when it is excessive in intensity or duration. A particular form of anxiety is that associated with exposure to certain relatively harmless environments such as walking in streets, being in open spaces, driving a car, or in crowded enclosed places. The term agoraphobia is now used to cover these specific anxieties, and the persistent avoidance of the trigger situations. Current research has focused upon the feeling of extreme panic, the panic attack, which is often associated with the development and experience of agoraphobia.

Agoraphobia generally begins after a period of mounting anxiety or stress which culminates in a panic attack. The individual develops an anticipatory fear of having such an attack and soon becomes reluctant to enter situations deemed likely to precipitate attacks. The prospect of a panic attack makes patients reluctant to leave safe surroundings, and normal activities become increasingly constrained by the fears and avoidance behaviours which come to dominate their lives. The situations which are most commonly avoided are travelling and being in crowds (for example, busy streets, crowded stores, tunnels, bridges, elevators, cars, buses, trains and aeroplanes). When avoidanced behaviour is complete, panic attacks may no longer be experienced as often, but at the cost of an inability to leave home alone. The severity of the disorder waxes and wanes, with periods of complete remission being possible. On bad days individuals may be housebound, whilst on good days they may be able to venture to the local shop (Burrows *et al.*, 1982; Molnar and Evans, 1983).

Although drug therapy, with anxiolytics, is the most frequent form of treatment used by psychiatrists when dealing with phobias, these same psychiatrists believe that some form of psychotherapy and real life exposure to the phobic situations should also be used (Burrows *et al.*, 1982). This paradoxical tendency to use a treatment other than the one regarded as the most appropriate is worthy of some comment. It has been suggested (Burrows *et al.*, 1982) that the tendency to use chemotherapy for agoraphobia may well be an expression of the urgency with which agoraphobics demand temporary relief from their attacks of anxiety. Thus, the use of drug therapy may be first interpreted as an indication that a rapid technique is needed.

There have been attempts to offer an alternative explanation to justify the use of drugs in this disorder (e.g. Sheehan, 1982). It has been suggested that some people are intrinsically susceptible to panic attacks. It is also accepted that the experience of a panic attack in somewhat threatening circumstances or simply in a place which is difficult to leave is the seeding event from which the subsequent phobia grows. It has been noted further that panic attacks are responsive to drug treatment, and from this observation it has been suggested that panic atacks must have a biological basis (Sheehan, 1982). This is reminiscent of the history of the lactate model of panic and anxiety which has been dismissed by history, and is discussed in Chapter 3. The simplistic interpretation that a drug-responsive symptom must have an underlying biological cause has obvious logical flaws, and these flaws have been noted: 'We must be aware that in complex systems, especially the brain, drugs may produce a therapeutic benefit by mechanisms that have little to do with the underlying cause of the disorder being treated' (Neubig, 1983, p. 342).

In summary, there is widespread use of chemotherapy for the anxiety of agoraphobia, but this reliance upon drugs is not based upon a demonstrated biological cause of the disorder, nor is it because chemotherapy is held in high regard by the practitioners who are prescribing the drugs. The agoraphobia sufferer appears to need urgent treatment, and to date psychological approaches do not appear to offer the necessary speedy symptomatic relief. With this summary of the problem in mind, a new hypnosis-based, psychological treatment for agoraphobia was designed.

This new agoraphobia treatment employs hyperventilation, or excessively heavy breathing. The belief that there is an association between hyperventilation and panic attacks is not new. Hyperventilation is mentioned in nearly every review of the panic attack or agoraphobia problem. Hyperventilation has been suggested as a cause, an intervening variable, and a result of panic attacks. It is widely accepted as being at least one of the factors which can contribute to panic and it has been described as one of the presenting signs with phobic patients (Van Dis, 1976; Magarian and Nardone, 1983).

Hyperventilation consists of rapid breathing which causes a decrease in extracellular CO_2 concentration, leading to respiratory alkalosis in the blood. Physiological effects include a decrease in the excitability of the threshhold peripheral nerves, chest pains, dizziness, and 'myriad of often pronounced and frightening symptoms' (Magarian and Nardone, 1983, p. 342). Hyperventilation is often associated with the precursor to phobias; the panic attack. Some interpretations suggest that hyperventilation is the cause rather than the product of these attacks (Lum, 1975). This proposition, implying that the response to a threat gets quite out of hand, has been summarized thus: 'the perception of threat is the first step into a vicious circle for some individuals, where increased ventilation, respiratory alkalosis, unpleasant body sensations, and increased apprehension elicit progressively stronger responses, often culminati.g in a panic attack' (Svebak and Grossman, 1985, p. 328).

The simplicity of this formulation of the panic attack, and presumably its link with the subsequent development of agoraphobia, has been challenged by direct experimentation. In an elegant experiment which measured personality variables, task demands, threat (from electric shock) and voluntary hyperventilation, a number of the complaints commonly elicited by and attributed to hyperventilation were recorded (Svebak and Grossman, 1985). The checklist of these complaints is given in Table 5. 1. In brief, it was found that for many people who present with hyperventilation-like complaints, the symptoms cannot be explained as being specifically due to hyperventilation. Instead, it appeared that the perception of a threatening context and the consequent elevation of 'apprehension' can also give rise to these symptoms *in the absence of overbreathing.* Even given these results, however, it was accepted that there almost certainly exists a significant population of 'psychosomatic hyperventilors' who experience the listed symptoms as a result of overbreathing. Most important for the present development of a means of controlling this type of anxiety response, the report by Svebak *et al* (1985) indicateJ that physical symptoms which are essentially identical with those of hyperventilation do occur in susceptible people during times of threat.

A quite different effect of hyperventilation, and one which has been almost totally ignored by recent literature, is that it can facilitate the induction of a hypnotic trance (Baykushev, 1969). Combining the propositions that hyperventilation is associated with panic attacks and that hyperventilation can aid the induction of a hypnotic trance, there is room to speculate that the noticed association between panic attacks and phobias may be evidence of a hypnotically augmented effect.

If panic attack, hyperventilation and agoraphobia are linked, the mechanism proposed here is that, at an earlier exposure to an unpleasant

Table 5.1. Psychosomatic signs of hyperventilation or panic attack*

Fits of crying
Unable to breathe deeply enough
Suffocating feeling
Rapid heartbeat
Feeling of unrest, panic
Tingling in feet
Nausea
Confused or dream-like feeling
Feeling of heat
Pounding of heart
Stomach cramps
Shivering
Irregular heartbeat
Tingling in legs
Feeling anxious
Chest pains around heart
Stiffness in fingers or arms
Cold hand or feet
Feeling head warmth
Tingling in arms
Stomach feels blown up
Knot in throat
Faster or deeper breathing than normal
Hands tremble
Dizziness
Tingling in fingers
Blacking out
Tenseness
Need for air
Fainting
Tiredness
Headaches
Tingling in face
Pressure in chest

*The psychosomatic complaints checklist should be scored on a four point scale:

never			very often
0	1	2	3

mean score = 17 (healthy university students). SD = 7.7.

situation, rapid breathing took place. This is an expected consequence of anxiety. This rapid breathing led to hyperventilation. Next, in addition to the initial level of anxiety, the unpleasant symptoms of hyperventilation could precipitate a panic attack (Magarian and Nardone, 1983). In line with our understanding of classical conditioning, the person might be expected to develop an association between the panic attack and the potentially phobic situation. Remembering that hyperventilation can aid in the production of a hypnotic trance, it was therefore reasoned that the potentially phobic patient undegoes a process of autohypnosis induction. Under hypnosis, a person has an enhanced tendency to make associations between events that are not necessarily related— that is, they 'learn' that one thing leads to another. The acquisition of phobic avoidance is an example of inappropriate learning where the person associates anxiety with a nonthreatening object, and also associates relief from anxiety with the act of avoiding the target of the phobia.

The last step in this sequence is that the anxiety-stimulated hyperventilation habit might induce a hypnotic state each time the feared situation was approached, and this would regularly add to the perceived frightening nature of the situation. The person would feel the sensations of loss of control, inability to think clearly, and quite excessive and traumatizing anxiety on each occasion. This is, of course, exactly what they report.

The above formulation of the problem is not only appealing in that it explains how all the observed symptoms and signs of agoraphobia are linked, it also offers a model upon which a treatment process can be designed. To review the mechanism we have suggested a chain of linked events involving an unpleasant stimulus situation, mild anxiety, hyperventilation, panic attack, and hypnosis-augmented classical conditioning to confirm the acquisition of the phobia. The key component in this chain is the hyperventilation procedure leading to a partial trance state and thus to an enhanced propensity for conditioning, or, in this case, faulty learning. Each of the steps in this explanation relies upon established psychological principles. Furthermore, the explanation is compatible with the finding that drug therapy, aimed at reducing the severity of the initiating state of stress, can indeed provide at least limited success in combating the phobic problem. The advantage of the present explanation is that it releases the proponents of drug therapy from the difficult position of advocating an explanation based upon an underlying biochemical defect in the patients. Under the proposed explanation, the effectiveness of drug therapy could be taken as evidence that a therapy which breaks into the sequence at any stage may be successful. The success of chemotherapy, would not be a reason for rejecting the search for a hypnosis-based management approach.

a. The management procedure

Based upon the above formulation of the problem, a treatment program involving hyperventilation as the trance-induction method has been developed. Much of the program uses relatively standard approaches of graded *in vivo* exposure, but it is novel in the speed with which relief is afforded. Rapid relief is obtained because part of the initiating sequence, hyperventilation, is now employed as a means of developing the new response of deep and satisfying relaxation.

In the past, breathing control has been suggested as a means for combating panic attacks, but these earlier methods have not taken advantage of the trance-producing potential of hyperventilation. A typical suggestion which draws attention to the suspected role of hyperventilation, but does not take advantage of the hypnotic possibilities might be: 'To alert the patient to the importance of hyperventilation. . . have the patient hyperventilate for up to three minutes whilst standing with eyes closed. This will allow him/her to identify early warning signs and progressive effects of hyperventilation. The test procedure should cease before severe symptoms occur' (Burrows *et al.*, 1982).

The new procedure is not simply a demonstration of hyperventilation. The patient should be given a short explanation of the effects of hyperventilation. He or she should be instructed to follow the therapist's instructions carefully, and shown how to breathe deeply. As hyperventilation progresses, suggestions concerning some of the usual signs such as dizziness and tingling in the hands or feet are made. For the best effect these suggestions should be timed so that they are presented shortly before the natural occurrence of the symptoms (Baykuschev, 1967). The patient should be instructed to indicate the onset of tingling in the fingers by a sign such as raising an index finger.

At the onset of such a symptom, the patient can be instructed to breathe naturally, and further deepening suggestions are made to take advantage of the very real contrast between the harsh and noisy hyperventilation period compared with the quiet, peaceful, relaxing, and mildly euphoric period which follows. To enhance control over the trance state, the following coding suggestion needs to be made: 'whenever you wish to deeply relax, just take one deep breath, then breathe out slowly and the same peaceful and calm state will return'.

A tape recording of this session, ending with the suggestion that the patient can remain relaxed and will gradually come to a normal state of complete alertness, feeling unusually calm during the following 15 minutes provides a good homework exercise for the patient to continue with.

After the first session, the patient should be instructed to practise with the tape, and to return for more specific therapy. After a week of practice with the tape, the patient usually responds well to the use of a rapid induction technique using just one deep breath, as coded in the tape. Future sessions can use the hyperventilation-induced trance to focus on the particular aspects of each patient's phobia.

The following case report indicates the treatment received by a 40 year old male patient whose case of panic attack had progressed to a stage where agoraphobia was a serious threat.

Dear Doctor,

Thankyou for seeing Robert, who needs help with managing his stress. This has been a problem over recent years, and appears related to his work as a Real Estate Agent, and to the travelling involved in the job.
He describes feelings of anxiety and somatic symptoms, particularly in traffic. He is concerned about his health, in particular his heart—a cardiograph was normal. He has benefited to some extent from antidepressant and anxiolytic drug therapy, but is understandably reluctant to continue these drugs long-term.

This referral note includes many of the components of a panic attack case. The most important point is the absence of recognition of the problem by the general practitioner. The assessment of heart function, other physical tests, and the real but limited value of drug therapy are all typical of the panic attack disorder. The association of panic attacks with a particular situation such as driving a car is also typical. Untreated, this problem would almost certainly have deteriorated into a serious case of agoraphobia and the patient would have become unable to continue with his work.

A clinical interview indicated that Robert had difficulties coping with criticism from his superviser. His physical signs included many of those on the symptom checklist in Table 5.1. He particularly mentioned the experience of pins and needles in the hands and arms.

It was decided to manage his case as primarily one of panic attack, although there was an additional component of anxiety arising from his irrational demands that his boss should not be unfair. The first clinical session therefore concluded with an introduction to the hyperventilation technique.

In the second week, specific suggestions were made relating to his ability to feel relaxed and calm whilst driving. A tape of this hypnosis sessions was made for repeated home use.

In many cases of panic attack, the therapy outlined above provides relief not only from the anxiety-provoking panic attack itself, but also gives the patient a sense of self-control which spreads to other potentially stressful areas of his or her life. However, the problem of Robert's inability to cope with criticism was a continuing source of anxiety, and so an intervention based upon Rational Emotive Therapy was introduced. The underlying irrational beliefs (people must be fair to me, etc.) were pointed out and challenged, and Robert was helped to change them.

Robert was about 20 kg overweight when he presented for therapy, and he did not actively exercise. He indicated that he would like to become fitter, and so a steadily increasing exercise program was suggested. Over the course of two months he adopted new exercise habits which included a gentle jog in the mornings before breakfast.

Over two months of therapy, Robert's progress was good. His panic attacks reduced in freqeuncy, as expected, within the first three weeks. Added to this he was making slow but consistent progress in changing his demands that his boss should never be 'unfair'. He was recommended a book by Ellis (1975) on the applications of Rational Emotive Therapy, and developed to a stage where he was able to challenge some of his own irrational emotional responses. It is not possible to comment upon what degree of benefit came from the exercise program, but he continued to run each morning and reported that this made him feel 'much better'.

As indicated above, many cases of panic attack respond very quickly to the general program which uses the hyperventilation-based hypnosis. Although most patients are believed by their referring doctor to have an 'anxiety problem' in only a few instances of panic attack is it necessary to include further therapy. Robert's case illustrates this.

Chapter 6
CONTROLLING AND USING STRESS

At first glance, the title of this chapter may seem confusing. The results and the theories presented so far seem to agree that stress is bad for you. It is easy to anticipate a section on controlling or reducing stress, but how could we imagine *using* it? There are two ways in which we can use stress. First, there is a special group of people who actually do thrive under stress. These people are often the most successful in business and in sport. We will see how these special people differ from 'normal', more vulnerable people. We will see that they are able to use stress to advantage. Second, since stress generally interferes with the way people perform then we can expect that our adversaries in sport, in business, and in life will be trying to stress us. In discussing this we will see how, in their attempts to become more efficient in the face of stress, present-day military systems are bringing us closer to the very serious stressor of world conflict. Back at an individual level of functioning, we will give guidance in the recognition of stress-inducing tricks. To help you get the upper hand in real-life contests, this chapter will present some of the tactics that can be used to cause stress in people. To give us a basis for this approach we will refer to the theoretical positions presented in Chapter 5.

A. REDUCING STRESS IN THE WORKPLACE

Combining the theories about people's beliefs with the experience of managing clinical problems we can begin to understand how it is possible to cause stress. We also gain knowledge of which steps might prevent it. Before some dramatic, new and amazingly different formulation of stress is anticipated, let us assert that the ideas which emerge from correct psychological interpretations of the situation are often remarkably similar to the inferences of commonsense. This is necessarily true. Psychology rarely comes up with a totally new formulation of the human situation, because the human situation is not new. The difference between psychology and commonsense is that commonsense includes a lot of things which are untrue whereas psychology has tested, studied, and refined 'commonsense'. The chaff has been removed from the grain and the residual advice is correspondingly more useful.

Let us now consider how those powerful defensive beliefs work against the onset of stress in real life. The three beliefs can be paraphrased as 'it can't happen to me', 'the boss will help', and 'my workmates are all behind me, we are all in this together'. To produce an atmosphere where these beliefs are supported, the individual factors that apply at a particular worksite must be considered. Here are some examples of their application.

The first belief can be eroded if there is a series of disasters which seem to pick off the workers one at a time. These disasters might be retrenchments, they might be industrial accidents, or they might be removal of workers from a favoured status (such as being on overtime, or chosen for an easy roster). If you are trying to create a mood of anxiety, which will probably lead to depression, hostility and anger, then try to instil the belief that 'it might happen to me'. But the resulting tension will not lead to high productivity or good attendance. To the contrary it will lead to stress, distractions in concentration, and increased industrial accidents. This prediction follows easily from our present undeestanding of stress, but it is not just a prediction; it is a fact. In a study involving nearly 3000 men in the United States Navy over a period of six years, it was found that the men with higher 'feelings of anxiety' also had higher rates of hospitalization, a poorer promotion record, and reduced productivity (Johnson et al., 1981). The study indicated that, for an individual in a state of chronic stress, the price paid by that individual is a poor promotion rate; the price that the organization pays is reduced efficiency and increased hospitalizations. This study demonstrated the difference between stressed and unstressed employees. There will always be some individuals who are more stressed than others, but if actions are taken to encourage the belief that 'the next victim might be me', then employees will suffer more stress and the organization will suffer poorer productivity.

The next defensive belief suggests that one's superiors will help in times of trouble. If there is prevailing economic hardship and union-backed conflict, it is of course difficult to instil the notion that help of any type will come from above. But, aside from particularly adverse conditions, do the workers in a particular area have the perception that they are being led by strong leaders they can rely on? Military studies often tell us much about the psychology of the masses. Officers and generals are, in the mind of the enlisted men, assigned the role of the omnipotent servant. The history of battles is studded with reports of high ranking officers who have rallied their men by appearing on the front and leading them. One example occurred at the Battle of Waterloo where the French Marshal Ney led unprotected horse cavalry against Wellington's cannon in five unsuccessful and immensely costly assaults. Ney earned the title of *la brave de la brave* for this inspirational effort. Nearly all of his men were killed. The soldiers were clearly operating under a delusional belief in their leader's omnipotence. During World War II, Rommel in the German Army, Montgomery for the British, and Macarthur with the United States Army achieved this image of imnipotence. However away from the special conditions that operate in wartime, it may not be so easy to achieve the same aura on the commercial or industrial front, but some of the actions which help the myth include regular appearances of superiors especially when or where things are difficult; appearing to be successful (not trying to be 'one of the boys (*sic*)'); making comments to indicate that you know exactly what someone is doing or precisely what the difficulties are; and looking quickly through a complicated document and then demanding an explanation of one particular point as if the rest had been totally absorbed and understood. The appearance of omniscience inspired by this last technique adds a great deal to a leader's apparent omnipotence.

The third defensive belief involved the idea that we are all in this together, and that we have community support for our actions. This community support might mean the greater community that we live in, or the community of fellow workers. In cases of industrial action, the community of fellow workers is most important in preventing worker anxiety. The belief that the community at large does not approve an action takes a long time to erode the strength of a union-backed campaign. In Britain, for example, in 1985 the national coal miners' strike lasted for nearly one year before widespread community disapproval appeared to curtail the powerful group support derived from union solidarity. The serious and long term deleterious effects of the withdrawal of community support is illustrated by the case of the veterans of the Vietnam war. These people now suffer an unusually high level of post-combat neurosis, apparently brought on by their dispersion in a community which strongly disapproved of the war and the way it was conducted. A focus for the resulting anxiety has been found in their obsession with Agent Orange (herbicide) effects on their health. The veterans experience high levels of chronic anxiety about 'physical complaints, including gastrointestinal disturbance, psychiatric problems, peripheral nerve disfunction, and cancer...' (LaVecchio *et al* 1983). While no studies have yet reported a systematic increase of abnormal physical symptoms, nor of birth defects (Kalter and Warkany, 1983) resulting from exposure to herbicides among Western soldiers who served in Vietnam, the returned soldiers continue to experience great anxiety in this regard. The fears about Agent Orange can be interpreted as an example of a neurotic response to chronic anxiety, the anxiety being due to the removal of the 'fellow worker' level of group support (repatriation from the army life) together with the clear evidence of community disapproval. The best 'cure' for Agent Orange neurosis would not be massive and grudgingly given compensation, but a serious indication that the returned soldiers now have community approval.

In summary, individuals in any organization will periodically suffer from stress. This is inevitable. But widespread feelings of stress can also arise and, when this is allowed to occur, reduced worker efficiency and increased physical ill-health will follow. One of the most important defences against the development of stress among a normal population is the fostering and supporting of the three beliefs outlined above. On the other hand, if even one of these beliefs is undermined, there is a serious risk of worker stress and an increase in stress related physical symptoms, absenteeism and claims for compensation. Can our society affords this?

B. 'GIANTS' WHO CAN USE STRESS

The stress–performance story so far has been in the form of a steadily growing mountain of evidence which showed that, on average, stress reduces performance. Theories predict this, studies confirm it, and our experience also supports the idea. But what does this mean for the individual? If we have an effect 'on average' it means that, in the absence of any other information, that is what we should expect more than half of the time. In the case of the stress–performance studies, the consistency and clarity of the results allow us to be certain that considerably more than half the population is affected badly by stress. But does this statistical prediction allow for any exceptions? And does our experience indicate that there are in fact any exceptions to the rule? The answer in both cases is 'yes'. The exceptions are relatively rare, but they are usually extremely successful in their fields of endeavour. They are emotional giants. They seem to do well under any circumstances, but they especially seem to thrive on stress. Who are they?

The first group of giants we encountered were players in the National League ice hockey competition in Finland. These men occupy a very special place in Finnish society. The desire to play at National League level is almost an obsession in each and every Finnish boy. The National League players are the few chosen from the many. From this elite of national players are selected the representatives for international competition—and resting on the shoulders of these representatives is the responsibility for defending the fierce national pride of 4.5 million Finns. Their opponents are numerical giants; the U.S.S.R. and U.S.A. The Finns often win, and they are always respected. But surely these men must suffer from stress. It is hard out there. They are against formidable opponents. Playing well is not good enough—after all who remembers second? Stress must occur, but it is not reasonable to suggest that stress could interfere with their performance. If we are going to find giants anywhere, we would find them here.

To assess the idea that giants were present in the ice hockey league, we repeated the 'soccer players and stress' experiment described in Chapter 2. Each player's number of hits (expressed relative to his time on the ice) was compared with his stress and arousal levels. Stress and arousal were measured by a carefully validated Finnish language form of the Linear Arousal and Stress Scale (LASS). This validation procedure is described elsewhere (King and Martin, 1986), and the descriptive statistics of the Finnish language version of the LASS are given in Chapter 4.

The experiment described in Chapter 2 showed that elevated levels of stress were associated with a reduced number of hits, while elevated levels of arousal tended to counter the otherwise bad effects of stress. However, the results from the top level ice hockey players showed that there was a consistent and significant improvement in performance as stress levels rose, the simple correlation between stress and number of hits being 0.49. This effect of stress is exactly in the opposite direction from that which our earlier experiments, and the literature, had indicated. This select group of men was quite unusual. They were indeed an example of the giants we were seeking; they were people who do better under stress.

There was a second way in which this group of giants was different from normal people. This was in their stress/arousal relationship. In Chapter 4 we discussed the concept that, although there is a range of different angles between stress and arousal, the average value is about 100°, corresponding to a small negative relationship (correlation coefficient approximately equal to − 0.2). For the Finnish National League ice hockey players, this angle was just 70°. This means that, although arousal was still a separate construct, for this group arousal had a tendency to rise in unison with stress. This seemed important. The data indicate that these giants were different in two ways. First, they played better under stress, and second they all tended to increase in arousal under stress.

Before this finding could be accepted as free from artifact, it would be necessary to show that all Finnish ice hockey players (or for that matter all

Finns) did not share these special characteristics. That is, this apparently unusual result might mean that all Finns have an angle of only about 70° between stress and arousal, and that all Finns are unperturbed by stress. To assess this possibility, a further study was conducted on a second division ice hockey team in Finland. The second division men were nominally identical with the first division players on all characteristics except one; they were not as good at ice hockey. These results replicated those found on the approximately second division level soccer players in Experiment 2.2; the second division ice hockey players performed worse under the effects of stress. Thus, the results from the second division players indicated that they were more representative of the normal population. Their performance had the expected negative relationship with stress, and, when their mood state data were examined, they were found to exhibit the more normal value of an average angle between stress and arousal of 100°.

To represent these propositions in a combined, mathematical expression, the computer was fed the individual stress/arousal angles for the men, together with measures of performance, stress, and arousal. The performance measures were best explained by a function of the type:

$$\text{performance} = a + \text{ST}\ (b + c^*\cos\theta)$$

where $\cos\theta$ is the cosine of the angle between each player's ST and AR value, and a, b, and c are constants. The multiple regression coefficient associated with this expression was 0.66, significant at better than 0.001 level.

The interpretation of the above formula is interesting. The formula means that two aspects of the player's moods are needed to explain the individual differences in performance. The first variable in the equation (ST) is a measure of the fluctuating mood state of the players during the game, and the second ($\cos\theta$) relates to a stable characteristic or trait of each man—the angle between stress and arousal which was introduced in Chapter 4.

The precise value of the constants (a, b, c) in the equation is not the point of interest here. These constants depend upon game-related factors such as the average number of hits for a player. The important issue is that the interactional theory of stress–arousal–performance has been further refined in this study. We have shown the existence of a group which thrives on stress, and we have called the members of this group giants. The results show that the giants differ from normal people on a measurable trait dimension; the angle relating stress and arousal. But very few people apart from the Finns aspire to be National League ice hockey players. Are there any other giants?

1. Are there giants of commerce?

An area which demands the highest level of performance from people, and which is generally regarded as being highly stressful, is management. In large organizations it is possible for demands to be created by people who are remote from those who must carry out the demands. This remoteness often leaves little opportunity for a person to negotiate task demands. This could mean that management personnel are under stress. For normal people, elevated levels of stress mean poorer performance. In economic terms poorer performance means inefficiency, reduced profitability, and wasted resources. But we now know that stress can have different effects as well. We have shown that there are giants who survive and indeed flourish under increase in stress. Is there any evidence that management giants exist?

Over the last decade there have been a number of reviews of stress in organizations (Beehr and Newman, 1978; Cooper and Marshall, 1976; Fletcher and Payne, 1980; Kasl, 1978; Sharit and Salvendy, 1982; van Sell *et al.*, 1981). The common theme of these reviews is that stress is due to a mismatch between the individual and the demands made of him or her. This finding is identical with the definition of stress adopted in this book. One of the most potent sources of this mismatch of resources and demands is the situation where an individual has the pressure of having too much to do in too little time. As if to emphasize this, an article has been published with the title 'Managing stress means managing time: the two are so intertwined that controlling one can only help the other' (Schuler, 1979).

The sort of arguments raised in such an article can be anticipated. Time is a resource of which the person has a limited quantity, and this resource may be partly under the control of someone else. The situation can arise where it is perceived that one has too little time for a task; that is there is a mismatch of demands and perceived resources. This will create stress. A stressed person might be expected to suffer a consequential reduction in ability, to take longer on tasks, or to make inappropriate decisions. Such a person will rapidly draw attention to him or herself, complaining frequently, becoming sick, seeking 'sideways' promotions, or ultimately leaving altogether. But the giants will remain. Is that the way it works in practice?

The proposition was tested in the marketplace (Cornwall, 1983). The business executives in a very large, nationwide retailing chain were studied in a stress evaluation program. The executives were assessed both by questionnaire and by personal interview about many stress-related areas including emotional problems, physical health complaints, and difficulties with interpersonal relationships. The questionnaire and the methodology have been described in full elsewhere (Cornwall, 1983).

From a factor analysis of the questionnaire, three groupings of items were distinguished. An abbreviated version of the text of each item is given in Table 6.1. An examination of the items found on the three scales suggested that they could be called 'stress', 'success' and 'failure'. The 'stress' grouping included the items which are generally found upon a broadly based stress inventory, as it includes indications of mood disorder itself together with signs of somatic aches, pains and complaints. The executives filled out the Stress/Arousal Check

List (SACL) (see Chapter 4) on just one occasion and, not surprisingly, the SACL stress scale score was related to the questionnaire 'stress' scale. These comparisons are given in Table 6.2. Considering the item content of the questionnaire 'stress' scale, it can easily be interpreted as indicating the results of negative, non-coping response to environmental demands.

Correlations between the questionnaire scales of arousal and arousal from the SACL (AR) were all relatively low. The correlations with arousal were in the direction to support the notion of AR as being a measure of coping response. The weakness of the AR correlations may be due in part to the sensitivity of this scale to moment to moment environmental demands.

As indicated, it was expected to find that one stress scale would compare well with a collection of stress-related complaints. But the comparisons with the SACL stress scale and the questionnaire responses in Table 6.2 show something of much greater interest. The so-called 'success' scale includes questions which related to time pressures. There were items to indicate that there was too little time to do all the required work, and that the work load was too high. With the same group were answers which indicated high job satisfaction, the feeling of having a clearly defined role, a high interest in the work, and feelings of doing the job well. High scores on this grouping of items went hand in hand (for most executives) with a low stress score, as indicated by the negative correlation between stress and 'success' in Table 6.2. This indication that time pressures are not necessarily stressful for men at the top is supportive of our belief in the existence of management giants.

Relevant to the present finding is the interpretation that has been given to other studies of stress in the workplace. For example, a recent report (Hoiberg, 1982) distinguished three occupational factors which were considered to place the individual under stress. These factors were environmental characteristics (physical demands, noise, temperature), job stressors (workload, responsibilities) and career considerations. Studies like this are quite common, and they have led to the reflex interpretation that workload and time pressures are inevitably sources of stress for everyone, including those in management. But this is not so.

When business executives are studied as a separate group their responses show that simply having high—even excessively high—time demands does not lead to stress. To the contrary it would seem that in order to select management giants and keep them interested in their work the pressure of too little time is vital. Evidence confirming the existence of giants can be found in other studies too. In an American study of the relationship between personal attitudes, conflict and stress (Steinmetz et al., 1982) there was a group of answers relating to apparently stressful complaints: 'management expects me to interrupt my work for new priorities', 'resource allocation in conflict', and 'others' demands upon me are in conflict'. As we have now learned to expect, managers who had these 'complaints' also had low stress scores.

Table 6.1. Items on the three scales from the Cornwall questionnaire (from Cornwall, 1983).

Stress	Success	Failure
headache	job satisfaction	physical conditions are bad
chest pain	work load high	difficulty delegating responsibility
aches and pain	interesting work	
lack of energy	too little time	compulsive eating
unable to get on with things	clearly defined role	
loss of interest	do job well	
irritability	get on with boss	
boredom	get on with colleagues	
problems relating	get on with subordinates	
depression		
tearfulness		
sexual problems		
loss of sexual desire		
memory problems		
blurred vision		
fatigue		
inability to think clearly		
presently experiencing stress		

Table 6.2. Correlation of ST and AR with (from SACL) scales from the Cornwall questionnaire.

scale	STRESS	SUCCESS	FAILURE
ST	.60	−.33	.07
AR	−.35	.18	−.29

Number of subjects = 79

Both the Cornwall (1983) study and the work of Steinmetz *et al.* (1982) show that a certain stratum of management is inhabited by people, both men and women, who can take stress. The management giants acknowledge the existence of pressures and impossible demands, they recognize the need to succeed, they know that no-one could meet these demands—but they feel great about it. Up until now these people have been largely self-selecting because we did not know what characteristics we were looking for. It was regularly found that people who do not fulfil the criteria and cannot become giants soon failed. In the authors' interviews with executives, some few who were not giants were present. These people reported depression, tearfulness, and problems relating to others; and their stress scores were high. The Steinmetz *et al*(1982) study also confirmed the existence of some people who, under the impossible time pressures imposed by the job, reported high stress, worry and depression, a tendency for self-blame and introspection, discomfort when speaking before a group, and difficulties communicating. Ordinary mortals do not fare well in giant country.

To conclude this section about organizational stress, it is unfortunate that too much of the writing about stress in business has been based upon theories evolved from research on normal people, or worse, people with psychological problems. This information has been woven into reports about stress in organizations but the reports have often been nothing more than a proliferation of trite, easily digested, trivial and unsupported utterances saying either that stress is due to excessive demands (from resources theory), or that an elusive optimum stress level which depends upon task difficulty should be achieved (inverted U theory), or that stress reduces performance ('normal people' theory). Given these vague and conflicting theories it has been difficult to make sense of the evidence from organizational research. Now it can be seen that the evidence is compatible with the theory of giants. There is a special breed of people who work well under pressure, and the more pressure the better. Belief in giants is not only supported by the evidence of psychological studies, it is also in accord with most peoples' experience of the market place.

C. USING STRESS AS A WEAPON

We have now seen that stress disrupts performance for most people and so it would be easy to conclude that you should never cause people to become stressed (aside from giants, that is). But life is a competition. Competitive situations arise all the time and in order to win we need to use every tool, every device, and every weapon. Can we use stress? Is stress used as a weapon already, and if so by whom?

We can learn at least a little about stress as a weapon from a study of military activities. The Soviet Union plans to use stress. At the border of the German Democratic Republic the Warsaw Pact forces have amassed enough artillary to mount an immensely heavy barrage of shells and rockets upon the enemy, the forces of NATO. In the case of a non-nuclear conflict this barrage would rain down upon the NATO troops. It is recognized that for properly dug in troops this barrage would inflict no more than 25% casualties, but it is also known that the remainder of the troops under this shock of shelling would be rendered immobile for at least two minutes after the cessation of shelling. This would be long enough for the rapid advance of Soviet tanks across the Western front line. The Soviet Army terms this acute stress response 'Battlefield paralysis'. They plan to avoid it themselves. This is interesting, but not easy to translate into everyday life, because there are laws about making excessive noise to disrupt your fellow competitors. But the Soviets study the application and avoidance of stress at lesser levels too.

The acute and severe reaction studied by the Soviets is related to more regularly occurring levels of stress 'by a continuum based on the severity, number and duration of. . . symptoms and their effect on the individual's ability to perform his (*sic*) duty' (Hibler and Duncan, 1983). Given this continuum it is logical to suppose that the Soviets plan for the existence of stress at lesser levels too. They recognize that everyone in a competitive situation may suffer from stress, and the Soviet summation of the problem is that 'The first casualty of stress. . . will be clear and reasoned thinking. The last to go. . . will be well rehearsed drills. It is here that drill and repetition score over intellect, wit and initiative' (Donnelly, 1982, p. 76). They advise against relying upon human decision making during competitive or military situations, and prefer to rely upon a carefully worked and detailed plan. This is not because of some insidious plan to dehumanize society, but simply for the very expedient reason that the Soviets believe in the disruptive powers of stress.

The first lesson about using stress, then, is that we might suffer from it ourselves. The second lesson is that, where possible, we should rely upon 'well rehearsed drills'. This will help to reduce stress effects in our own performance. But what about raising stress levels in others? It is true that if a person doubts his or her own ability, stress will probably rise and performance will suffer. Working from this self-evident truth, we often find 'backyard psychologists' or coaches of children's sporting teams shouting insults at the opposition and suggesting that they are in some way inadequate. It does not work. The opposition does not believe it, and they do not adopt these negative thoughts as their own. To use stress effectively we need to be more subtle than this.

From the studies of the irrational thought patterns reviewed in Chapter 5, there are two main themes which virtually guarantee the elevation of stress levels. They are thoughts which use the notions 'should' or 'shouldn't', and ideas that things are 'unfair'. In practice this translates into the need for an individual to do something unexpected, something which is not approved of, something which although not being against the letter of the law is clearly outside the (assumed) spirit of it. Some present-day tennis players provide a ready example of this. When they are beginning to lose, they suddenly commence a barrage of abuse at the umpire or the linesman. For success, this needs to be more than just a comment which indicates displeasure. The 'unsporting' behaviour must be so gross, so prolonged, and so unreasonable that any fairminded person would surely think 'he shouldn't be allowed to do that' or 'this is really unfair, just when my serves were going perfectly'. These are correct responses. He shouldn't do it, and it is unfair, but it works nearly every time.

Of course, to convert the opponent's stress into a win the unfair player must be a person of great talent as well.

Before your next sporting competition, go over the list of irrational beliefs. Then make a list of all the things that are 'unfair', that one absolutely 'shouldn't do', and then do them (or at least do the worst of them). If your opposition is not upset and stressed so by this behaviour, then perhaps you have not been unfair enough, so try harder. There is only one way to be nice, but rudeness has a thousand faces. The same advice would apply to a business confrontation where some concession is being negotiated, or where you are trying to outstage a colleague. If the others are thinking your behaviour is 'unfair' you are half-way there, but remember that the other half depends upon your talent and your preparation. However, be warned; only use these techniques if you want to win. If you just want to be liked, take up aerobics.

1. Colour as a weapon

Throughout much of this century the effects of colour upon mood have been the subject of study by psychologists. The results of these studies have been either ignored totally, or misquoted drastically by charlatans trying to make money. People committing these frauds have included interior decorators, clothing designers, and 'colour therapists' who claim to help your psychological well-being through the use of certain colour-related prescriptions.

In the first place, ideas about colour and mood came from intuitive interpretations by artists. Gradually over this century these interpretations have been verified by the results of experiments. Experiments relating to mood and colour have always involved short-term exposure to fairly strong colours for between five minutes and half an hour in a room, an enclosure or a painted booth. The mood of the person so exposed was sometimes assessed by simple questions, and sometimes by more formalized psychological tests. For instance, using Spielberger's State Anxiety scale it was found that five minutes exposure to red elevated levels of anxiety (Jacobs and Suess, 1975). Where arousal has been measured levels have been generally found to be elevated by yellows (Greene et al., 1983), and yellow also is associated with happiness (Peretti, 1974). The shorter wavelength end of the spectrum, particularly the blues, are usually not as stimulating either for anxiety or arousal; blue-violet has been reported to create a sense of sadness and fatigue (Levy, 1980). Sometimes blue and green have been found to give a sense of calmness and quietness (Jacobs and Suess, 1975), but green has also been singled out as causing feelings of anger (Levy, 1980).

In trying to make sense of the literature on these effects, the first problem is that, as in many other 'stress' experiments, both stress and arousal were rarely measured. Where measurements of mood were made or at least hinted at in terms that we can interpret there is a consistent trend indicating that red causes anxiety and anger. Yellow appears to be associated most often with higher arousal and positive feelings, and, as we move towards blue, the associated moods seem to be progressively lower, that is, definitely not aroused and perhaps not anxious either. The depression associated with violet–blue would be a state interpreted in psychological terms as combining anxiety with low arousal. This finding is reasonable from a colorimetric point of view, too, since violet occupies the position on the colour circle which links the short wavelength blue colours with the long wavelength reds. Blue relates to sadness and low arousal; red causes anxiety.

Before commenting upon the practical application of colour–mood effects, it should be noted that the only respectable studies published showing an effect of colour on mood used short-term exposure to strong shades. This is not surprising to the psychologist. The effect of colour, although it is real, is relatively subtle. Humans habituate quite quickly to even very powerful and disruptive conditions, and therefore the more gentle forces of colour must soon fade. It is not possible to create a permanent mood by painting the office or factory a certain colour. If it has an effect at all, the effect will not last more than a few days. But there is a place where this research could be applied, and that is in a room where a colleague, or an adversary, must wait immediately before your meeting or contest. In the business setting, this could mean a waiting room; in sport it could be the visitors' dressing room. If your competitor is a giant, avoid colours such as red which elevate stress and arousal—this is just what giants need. The safest colours for disrupting the opposition appear to be blues and violets. Choose yellows to stimulate the arousal levels of your own team. Whatever you do with this knowledge, be aware that the effects of colour are relatively subtle, and probably only last for a short time. Be prepared to move quickly to take advantage of that brief period.

D. STRESS AND HUMAN SURVIVAL

Stress has always affected people, and its effects have generally been bad. Despite this, the human race has survived. Things have now changed and stress, or the consequences of stress, may help to eliminate our world. The last word in this book is therefore a warning.

We have seen so far that stress can affect people in all occupations. Stress can affect their decision making processes. We have further seen that at least some military planners are aware that the effects of stress can interfere with their tactics. Strategies have been made to minimize the effects of stress on their own forces, or to maximize the effects of stress on the 'enemy'. This knowledge should make the reader feel comfortable: our defenders are prepared to function under stress. The studies of stress have been turned into practical lessons, and the military system has instituted a program of well-learned drills which can be carried out even under frighteningly stressful conditions. This means that under conditions of perceived threat the members of the military forces have a quite limited repertoire of responses available to them, so that they will not be required to make difficult decisions.

The effects of stress, with their consequent impact upon decision making, are felt by men and women in the ranks and officers alike. Indeed Bourne (1969) found that the levels of stress were apparently greater among the decision makers during military operations. We have established that under conditions of stress normal intellectual functions are interfered with, and therefore even within the restricted range of options which are available to the military decision maker, an even more impoverished potential range will have been included in his or her final selection. To a deliberate and very real extent the Warsaw Pact commanders accept that, under stress, competent decision making will suffer. Therefore in battle, or under the threat of hostility, military decisions should not rely on reasoned decisions. Whilst the NATO attitude is not quite so dogmatic and the process of reasoned decision making is not specifically banned, the training of military decision-makers from junior officer status upwards leads to a somewhat similar result.

The junior officers obtain their tactical experience in special execises: Tactical Exercises Without Troops, or TEWTs. The exercises deliberately provide a highly complex situation with many variables, or, in psychological terms, 'information overload'. Early experiences in these exercises indicate to the young officer that he or she cannot logically analyse the situation, dealing with all the variables (Hellyer, 1983; King et al., 1984). There are relatively few variables which the human mind can successfully manipulate and an attempt to operate in an overload situation will necessarily yield a solution which contains logical flaws, and which ignores a number of salient points. The only way to deal with an overload situation is to group the information into prelearned packages and thus reduce the load on the mind. This process of grouping data can render a highly complex multivariate problem into one which requires that a choice be made between very few solutions. In the world of business, we call this relying on experience. In the military, it is more correctly interpreted as reliance upon the lessons of a few well learned drills.

This process of limiting options continues throughout an officer's military career. Its consequences permeate all ranks. The young infantry soldier is taught that 'the role of infantry is to seize ground, and to hold it . . .' This overlearned definition of the role of infantry only considers the inevitability of conflict and of hostile military action. This typifies the range of options which are present in the minds of our defenders. It could be, not unfairly, represented as offering choices between 'firing gun A, firing gun B, or firing both A and B'.

It is not all that unusual to limit the number of responses between which a trained professional chooses. Psychologists, for example, are trained in a way which limits the extent of the domain from which their decisions come, and the sort of actions they will take. One would not expect to find a clinical psychologist who considered an astrological explanation of depressive symptoms, although perhaps a more open-minded, or untrained, person might not exclude this possibility. We are all limited by our training and our experience. We cannot afford the luxury of redefining each new case from first principles. We operate on a relatively limited number of responses taken from a gamut of interpretations which itself is also restricted. We cannot, and we do not, think of everything or every possibility. This in itself is not wrong. Most professions, including that of psychology, are subject to a range of criticisms which come from within the professional body and also from the people we deal with. Economic forces also tend to keep most of us within somewhat sensible limits. If we are too unsuccessful, or simply wrong most of the time, we will not survive.

Overall most professions are required to produce results which are satisfactory to the public, and also satisfactory to the person whom our actions have affected. Although we are not perfect, we hope to become 'righter and righter' because of this opportunity for feedback. In the case of military training, however, the situation is quite different. There is no deliberate regard for what the general public might regard as good or bad. There is even less regard for the opinions of the people upon whom military decisions operate; they are called the enemy. In the absence of this feedback loop to bring in criticisms from outside the body itself, the system could become 'wronger and wronger'. Each unit within the military system tends to act in accordance with its own set of rules and goals. The goals for each operating unit are usually set by a higher military level of command, but the responsibility for the prescription of goals and the methods of attaining them still remains within the military system. At the highest level, political instructions might appear to generate the subsequent military action, but the political instructions are based upon choices offered by military advisers.

Thus we have an organization which, in order to protect itself from the deleterious effects of stress, has deliberately fostered a process of limiting the range of decisions available in any given action. We also have a situation where the military system is more or less deliberately insulated from feedback about the rightness of its actions. The decisions made are only choices between different styles of hostility. That these military decisions often have no military value in a broad sense, and are equally devoid of political advantage, can be seen in many decisions taken during military crises—that is, in decisions taken under stress. The interested reader can turn to virtually any military history to find examples of appalling blunders, all with the consequence of slaughter on a massive scale.

A case can certainly be made to show that military leaders are often incapable of making rational decisions whilst subjected to the stressor of military action. Perhaps these catastrophes could be taken as evidence that it is correct to limit decision making opportunities. However, bear in mind that in order to avoid foolish decisions military organizations have limited the range of choices to a selection between very few hostile actions. Assuming that we do not really want further global conflict, is this stress-avoidance technique really the way to peace? In fact the military machines of both the U.S.S.R. and U.S.A. (representing the dominant forces in the Warsaw Pact and NATO, respectively) have both shown themselves to be incapable of making any other than a hostile response when action is requested. This is the case even when the action is requested in a non-threatening situation. Examples are legion, and fresh ones can be regularly noticed. Here we will consider just two.

The first example of the Gun A or Gun B philosophy is demonstrated in the Korean airliner 'disaster' where a Soviet fighter shot down an unarmed civilian passenger airliner. This was not a hasty decision, nor one made under stress, but it shows the danger of the present stress-avoidance strategy. The missile was fired not when the airliner entered restricted airspace, but only after the aircraft had intruded for about two hours. There was evidence of messages passing across the continental mass of the Soviet Union, evidence that the decision was considered at a high level. There was apparently no 'Option C' in the Soviet rule book—don't shoot at all—only the Gun A or Gun B options. The incident has been analysed at length elsewhere (Westlake, 1983), but in no analysis has it been suggested that either a political or a military advantage was anticipated when the decision was made to shoot. No advantage in fact appeared to follow.

The second incident to be considered is the military response by the United States to the terrorist suicide truck-bomb which demolished the United States Embassy in Beirut, Lebanon. There were a significant number of casualties. About 24 hours later, the United States military command authorised the shelling of suspected terrorist positions. The bombardment came from ships stationed offshore. The U.S.A. announced that it had no option but to embark upon this shelling procedure. Perhaps there was no option under the Gun A or Gun B principle. The tangible fact was that the level of shelling which resulted represented only a relatively light assault in military terms. In practice minimal casualties would have been caused on a conventional concentration of troops, but in this case the targets were not precisely defined, but were simply places where terrorists might happen to be. The main military goal of shelling is to restrict enemy movement until a ground-based assault can be mounted, but this United States action was not acompanied by any such offensive. It probably represented a minor nuisance to the 'enemy'. Of course for any civilians upon whom the shells landed, the result was no doubt far more than a minor nuisance—and the noise must have been awful. Perhaps this response could be best interpreted as Gun A *and* Gun B. In any case, no military advantage could have been anticipated, and none was claimed. A corresponding absence of political advantage appeared to come from the action too.

These two cases have been cited to indicate the severe limitation of the military decision gamut, a limit that is present even when there is no actual threat to the decision makers, a limit that restricts their decisions to a selection between a few manifestly foolish actions even when there is plenty of time to consider the situation in detail. There are two important lessons to be learned from this study of the military approach to dealing with stress.

The first lesson is that if we limit our decisions to a few well-learned drills we probably will be able to function better under stress, but the drills might not include the best decision. The drills might not even include an *appropriate* decision. This lesson has application in real life areas, including sport and business preceders. It should also be heeded by individual members of the helping professions, who may inadvertanly lean towards a strategy akin to the military approach, to reduce the deleterious effects of stress on their performance.

The second lesson is at once philosophical, and yet very applied. It is that the nature and process of the military procedure is in question. If the leading officers are steadily refined by an unforgiving system that allows only for Gun A or Gun B solutions, it is only to be expected that this is the type of military advice that our political leaders will be offered. The total military training package will not of course be abandoned, nor should it be. It produces very professional warriors. However, surely it is possible, in the interests of world peace, to include consideration of the peaceful Option C in the gamut of available decisions for each exercise. In assessment, it would seem better that bonus marks be given to a young officer who profers a response which involves no hostility at all.

It will be 20 years before today's officer cadets reach the rank of major. Only the most orthodox of these young men (or women) will become generals. If our proposed peaceful solution to military problems is to be suggested by generals, it will need to have been an orthodox and acceptable solution for at least 20 years. Of course, we may not have 20 years or more remaining before the Gun A/Gun B option leads us into terrible trouble. We can consider it fortunate that medicine, business, sport, and psychology are not that inflexible.

E. EPILOGUE

The effects of stress upon people are real and important. It is correspondingly important for everybody to understand these effects, to prepare for them, to avoid them, and to use them wisely. One way of avoiding the effects of stress is to never make original decisions, but we have shown that this approach can have disadvantages and it could lead to the end of the world.

Our present state of knowledge indicates that stress interferes with performance by disrupting concentration. Increased arousal serves to protect against this effect of stress. The study of stress is continuing, and clearer interpretations will come from further experiments.

For the moment, however, the authors recognize the need for a clear and practical summary of the stress story as far as it is understood today. To provide for this need we have tried to write a book which could be read and valued by everyone. We also intended to stimulate further questions and to encourage the search for further answers.

REFERENCES

Abraham P. Training for battleshock. *Journal of the Royal Army Medical Corps* 1982, *128*, 18-27.

Ackerman SA and Sachar EJ. The lactate theory of anxiety: a review and re-evaluation. *Psychosomatic Medicine* 1974, *36*, 69-81.

Antelman SM and Rowland N. Endogenous opiates and stress-induced eating. *Science* 1981, *214*, 1149.

Atkinson JH, Kremer EF, Risch SC, Morgan CD, Azad RF, Ehlers CL, and Bloom FE. Plasma measures of beta-endorphin/beta-lipotropin-like immunoreactivity in chronic pain syndrome and psychiatric subjects. *Psychiatry Research* 1983, *9*, 319-327.

Baddeley AD. Selective attention and performance in dangerous environments. *British Journal of Psychology* 1972, *63*, 537-546.

Bagley RT. Relationship of diet to physical/emotional complaints and behavioural problems reported by women students. *Journal of Orthomolecular Psychiatry* 1981, *10*, 284-298.

Baumeister RF. Choking under pressure: Self consciousness and paradoxical effects of incentives on skillful performance. *Journal of Personality and Social Psychology* 1984, *46*, 610-620.

Baykushev SV. Hyperventilation as an accelerated hypnotic induction technique. *International Journal of Clinical and Experimental Hypnosis* 1969, *17*, 20-24.

Beehr TA and Newman JE. Job stress, employee health and organizational effectiveness: A facet analysis, model, and literature review. *Personnel Psychology*, 1978, *31*, 665-669.

Bell PA. Physiological, comfort, performance, and social effects of heat stress. *Journal of Social Issues* 1981, *37*, 71-94.

127

Bergstrom B. The effect of sleep loss and threat-induced stress upon tracking. *Scandinavian Journal of Psychology* 1972, *13*, 54-60.

Berlyne DE. *Conflict, Arousal and Curiosity*. New York: McGraw-Hill, 1960.

Bills AG. Blocking: A new principle in mental fatigue. *American Journal of Psychology* 1931, *43*, 230-245.

Bills AG. Some causal factors in mental blocking. *Journal of Experimental Psychology* 1935, *18*, 172-185.

Bohlin G and Kjellberg A. Self reported arousal during sleep deprivation and its relation to performance and physiological variables. *Scandinavian Journal of Psychology* 1973, *14*, 78-86.

Bohlin G and Kjellberg A. Self-reported arousal. *Scandinavian Journal of Psychology* 1975, *16*, 203-208.

Borkovec TD. Insomnia: a review. *Journal of Consulting and Clinical Psychology* 1982, *50*, 880-895.

Bourne PG (ed.). *The Psychology and Physiology of Stress.* New York: Academic Press, 1979.

Breakwell GM, Collie A, Harrison B, and Propper C. Attitudes towards the unemployed: Effects of threatened identity. *British Journal of Social Psychology* 1984 *21*, 87-88.

Broadbent DE. Noise, paced performance and vigilance tasks. *British Journal of Psychology* 1953, *44*, 295-303.

Broadbent DE, Cooper P, Fitzgerald P, and Parkes K. The cognitive failures questionnaire and its correlates. *British Journal of Clinical Psychology* 1982, *21*, 1-16.

Broadhurst PL. The interaction of task difficulty and motivation: The Yerkes Dodson Law revisited. *Acta Psychologica* 1959, *16*, 321-337.

Brown MG and Page J. The effect of chronic exposure to cold on temperature and blood flow of the hand. *Journal of Applied Physiology* 1952, *5*, 211-227.

Burrows GC, Cox T, and Simpson GC. The measurement of stress in a sales training situation. *Journal of Occupational Psychology* 1977, *50*, 45-51.

Burrows GD, Evans L, Franklin J, and Hafner J. A treatment outline for agoraphobia. *Australian and New Zealand Journal of Psychiatry* 1982, *16*, 25-33.

Campbell DT and Fiske DW. Convergent and discriminant validation by the multitrait-multimethod matrix. *Psychological Bulletin* 1959, *56*, 81-105.

Chan CSW. The psychological effects of running loss upon consistent runners. *Dissertation Abstracts International* 1981, *46*, 06, 2520.

Christie MJ and Chesher GB. Physical dependence on physiologically released endogenous opiates. *Life Sciences* 1982, *30*, 1173-1177.

Clark DE, Foulds A, Brown DM. *et al.* Serum urate and cholesterol levels in Air Force Academy cadets. *Aviation, Space and Environmental Medicine* 1975, *46*, 1044-1048.

Cohen ME and White PD. Life situations, emotions and neurocirculatory asthenia (anxiety neurosis, neurasthenia, effort syndrome). *Proceedings of the Association for Research in Nervous and Mental Disease* 1950, *29*, 832-869.

Cohen S and Spacapan S. The aftereffects of stress: An attentional interpretation. *Environmental Psychology and Nonverbal Behaviour* 1978, *3*, 43-57.

Collison DR. Hypnosis and respiratory disease. in GD Burrows and L Dennerstein (eds). *Handbook of Hypnosis and Psychosomatic Medicine.* New York: Elsevier/North Holland, 1977.

Colliver R and Farnell L. Reduced stress means a reduction in accidents. *Australian Safety News*, 1983, *54(1)*, 30-36.

Cooper CL and Marshall J. Occupational sources of stress: A review of the literature relating to coronary heart disease and mental ill-health. *Journal of Occupational Psychology* 1976, *49*, 11-28.

Cornwall J. Studies in organizational stress. Melbourne: University of Melbourne (unpublished report), 1983.

Cotton JL. A review of research on Schachter's theory of emotion and misattribution of arousal. *European Journal of Social Psychology* 1981, *11*, 365-397.

Cox T. *Stress.* Macmillan, Melbourne: 1978.

Csikszentmihalyi M. *Beyond Boredom and Anxiety.* Jossey-Bass, San Francisco: 1975.

Dahlstrom WG, Welsh GS, and Dahlstrom LE. *An MMPI Handbook.* Minneapolis: University of Minnesota Press, 1975.

Davies BM. *An Introduction to Clinical Psychiatry.* Melbourne: Melbourne University Press, 1973.

De Bruijn R. Deep transverse friction; its analgesic effect. *International Journal of Sports Medicine* abstract service presented at: International Congress on Sports and Health. Maastricht, The Netherlands, 1983.

Deffenbacher JL. Worry, emotionality and task-generated interference in test anxiety: an empirical test of attention theory. *Journal of Educational Psychology* 1978, *70*, 248–254.

Donnelly C. The Society Attitude to Stress in Battle. *Journal of the Royal Army Medical Corps* 1982, *128*, 72–78.

Duller P and Gentry WD. Use of biofeedback in treating chronic hyperhidrosis: A preliminary report. *British Journal of Dermatology* 1980, *103*: 143–6.

Ellis A. *A New Guide to Rational Living.* Englewood Cliffs, NJ: Prentice Hall, 1975.

Elton D and Stanley G. Cultural expectations and psychological factors in prolonged disability. In JL Sheppard (ed.) *Advances in Behavioural Medicine Vol 2* Sydney: Cumberland College of Health Sciences, 1982.

Feather NT. Unemployment and its psychological correlates: A study of depressive symptoms, self-esteem, Protestant Ethic values, attributional style, and apathy. *Australian Journal of Psychology* 1982, *34*, 309–323.

Fletcher B and Payne R. Stress and work: A review and theoretical framework. *Personnel Review* 1980, *9*, 19–29.

Freedman RR and Sattler HL. Physiological and psychological factors in sleep-onset insomnia. *Journal of Abnormal Psychology* 1982, *91*, 380–389.

Freud S. *Inhibitions, Symptoms and Anxiety*, London: Hogarth Press, 1961.

Fryer D and Warr P. Unemployment and cognitive difficulties *British Journal of Clinical Psychology* 1984, *23*, 67–68.

Fuerst ML. Insomniacs give up stress and medications. *Journal of the American Medical Association* 1983, *294*, 459–460.

Girodo M and Roehl J. Cognitive preparation and coping self-talk: Anxiety management during the stress of flying. *Journal of Consulting and Clinical Psychology* 1978, *46*, 978–989.

Glover V, Reveley MA, and Sandler M. A monoamine oxidase inhibitor in human urine. *Biochemist and Pharmacology* 1980, *28*, 467–470.

Gold MS, Pottash AC, Sweeny DR. *et al.* Opiate withdrawal using clonidine: A safe, effective and rapid nonopiate treatment. *Journal of the American Medical Association* 1980, *243*, 343–346.

Graham JR. *The MMPI: A Practical Guide.* New York: Oxford University Press, 1977.

Gray JA. Anxiety as a paradigm case of emotion. *British Medical Bulletin* 1981, *37*, 193–197.

Greene TC, Bell PA, and Boyer WN. Coloring the environment: Hue, arousal and boredom. *Bulletin of the psychonomic society* 1983, *21*, 253–254.

Gross T and Mastenbrook M. Examination of the effects of state anxiety on problem-solving efficiency under high and low memory conditions. *Journal of Educational Psychology* 1980, *72*, 605–609.

Haslam DR, Allnut MF, *et al.* The effects of continuous operations upon military performance of the infantryman. London: Ministry of Defence (unpublished Memorandum), 1977.

Hennessy JW and Levine S. Stress, arousal and the pituitary-adrenal system: A psychoendochrine hypothesis. *Progress in Psychobiology* 1979, *8*, 133–178.

Heuser J. Differential stress in problem solving. *Zeitschrift für Experimentelle und Angewandte Psychologie.* 1978, *25*, 379–406.

Healey ES, Kales A, and Monroe LJ. Onset of insomnia: Role of life-stress events. *Psychosomatic Medicine* 1981, *43*, 439–451.

Hellyer G. The study of tactics. *Defence Force Journal* 1983, *38*, 3–12.

Hellstrom B, Berg K, and Lorentzen FV. Human peripheral rewarming during exercise in the cold. *Journal of Applied Physiology* 1979, *29*, 191–199.

Hibler RJ and Duncan BJ. Battlefield stress management. *Medical Service Digest* 1983, *34*, 11-13.

Hockey R and Hamilton P. The cognitive patterning of stress states. In R Hockey (ed.). *Stress and Fatigue in Human Performance.* New York: Wiley, 1983.

Hoehn-Saric R, Merchant AF, Keyser ML, and Smith VK. Effects of clonidine on anxiety disorders. *Archives of General Psychiatry* 1981, *38*, 1278-1282.

Holmgren A and Strom G. Blood lactate concentration in relation to absolute and relative workload in normal men, in mitral stenosis, atrial septal defect and vasoregulatory asthenia. *Acta Medica Scandanavica* 1959, *163*, 189-193.

Howard L, Reardon JP, and Tosi D. Modifying migraine headache through rational stage directed hypnotherapy: A cognitive-experiential perspective. *The International Journal of Clinical and Experimental Hypnosis* 1982, *30*, 257-269.

Insel TR and Pickar D. Naloxone administration in obsessive-compulsive disorder: Report of two cases. *American Journal of Psychiatry* 1983, *140*, 1219-1220.

Jacobs KW and Suess JF. Effects of four psychological primary colours on anxiety state. *Perceptual and Motor Skills* 1975, *41*, 207-210.

Johnson LC and Spinweber CL. Good and poor sleepers differ in navy performance. *Military Medicine* 1983, *148*, 727-731.

Jones HG. Learning and Abnormal Behaviour. In HJ Eysenck (ed.). *Handbook of Abnormal Psychology.* Tunbridge Wells: Pitman, 1960.

Jones M and Mellersh V. A comparison of the exercise response in anxiety states and normal controls. *Psychosomatic Medicine* 1946, *3*, 180-187.

Kasl S. Epidemiological contributions to the study of work stress. in CL Cooper and R Payne (eds.). *Stress at Work.* New York: John Wiley, 1978.

Kasl SV, Cobb S, and Brooks GW. Changes in serum uric acid and cholesterol levels in men undergoing job loss. *Journal of the American Medical Associaiton* 1968, *205*, 1500-1507.

Kathol RG, Winokur G, Sherman BM, Lewis D, and Schlesser M. Provocative endocrine testing in recovered depressives. *Psychoneuroendocrinology* 1984, *8*, 57-67.

Kearns NP, Cruikshank CA, McGuigan KJ, Riley SA, Shaw SP, and Snaith RP. A comparison of depression rating scales. *British Journal of Psychiatry* 1982, *141*, 45-49.

Kalter H and Warkany J. Congenital malformations: Etiologic factors and their role in prevention. *New England Journal of Medicine* 1983, *308*, 424-431.

King MG and Campbell IM. A manifest anxiety scale from MMPI-168. *Journal of Clinical Psychology.* 1986, *42*, 748-750.

King MG and Martin J. Measurement of stress and arousal in Swedish and Finnish. Melbourne: University of Melbourne (unpublished report), 1986.

King MG and Symons MR. The effects of stress and arousal on performance. Melbourne: University of Melbourne (unpublished report), 1985.

King MG, Burrows GD, and Stanley GV. Measurement of stress and arousal: Validation of the stress/arousal adjective check list. *British Journal of Psychology* 1983, *74*, 473-479.

King MG, Stanley GV and Burrows GD. Visual search processes in camouflage detection. *Human Factors*, 1984a, *26*, 223-234.

King MG, Stanley GV, and Burrows GD. Stress, Combat and tactical decisions. *Defence Force Journal* 1984b, *44*, 9-15.

Kjellberg A. Sleep deprivation and some aspects of performance. *Waking and Sleeping* 1977, *1*, 139-153.

Klein DF, Zitrin CM, and Woerner MG. Antidepressants, anxiety, panic and phobia. In MA Lipton, A DiMascio and KF Killem (eds.). *Psychopharmacology: A Generation of Progress.* New York: Raven Press, 1978.

Kosten TR, Jocobs S, Mason J, Wahby V, and Atkins S. Psychological correlates of growth hormone response to stress. *Psychosomatic Medicine* 1984, *46*, 49-58.

La Vecchio FA, Hermine MP, and Singer W. Agent orange and birth defects. *New England Journal of Medicine* 1983, *308*, 719–720.

Leddwidge B. Run for your mind: Aerobic exercise as a means of alleviating anxiety and depression. *Canadian Journal for Behavioural Science* 1980, *12*, 126–140.

Lerer B and Jacobowitz. Treatment of Essential Hyperhidrosis. *Psychosomatics* 1981, *22*, 536–8.

Levy BI. Research into the psychological meaning of color. *American Journal of Art Therapy* 1980, *19*, 87–91.

Lievens P and Leduc A. Cryotherapy and sports. *International Journal of Sports Medicine* abstract service presented at: International Congress on Sports and Health. Maastricht, The Netherlands. 1983.

Linehan DL. *Repetition Strain Injury in the Australian Public Service.* Canberra: Australian Government Publishing Service, 1985.

Linko E. Lactic acid response to muscular exercise in neurocirculatory asthesia. *Annales de Medecine Interne Finne* 1950, *36*, 161–176.

Lipson A. Agent orange and birth defects. *New England Journal of Medicine* 1983, *309*, 492.

Lorr M and McNair DM. *Profile of Mood States: Bi-Polar Form.* San Diego: Educational and Industrial Testing Service, 1984.

Luck P and Wakeling A. Altered thresholds for thermoregulatory sweating and vasodilation in anorexia nervosa. *British Medical Journal* 1980, *281*, 906–908.

Lum LC. Hyperventilation: The tip and the iceberg. *Journal of Psychosomatic Research* 1975, *19*, 375–383.

Lyman B. The nutritional values of food group characteristics of foods preferred during various emotions. *Journal of Psychology* 1982, *112*, 121–127.

McCaffrey TV, Wurster RD, Jacobs HK, Euler DE and Geis GS. Role of skin temperature in the control of sweating. *Journal of Applied Physiology: Respiratory Environmental and Exercise Physiology* 1979, *47(3)*, 591–597.

Mackay C, Cox T, Burrows G and Lazzerini T. An inventory for the measurement of self-reported stress and arousal. *British Journal of Social and Clinical Psychology* 1978, *17*, 283–284.

Mackworth NH. Stimulus density limits the useful field of view. In RA Monty and JW Senders (eds). *Eye Movements and Psychological Processes.* Hillsdale, NJ: Lawrence Erlbaum Associates, 1976.

McNair DM, Lorr M, and Droppleman LF. *Profile of Mood States Manual.* San Diego: Educational and Industrial Testing Service. 1981.

McPhee B. *The Mechanism of Repetition Strains.* Canberra: Commonwealth Institute of Health, 1980.

McPhee B. The prevention and management of repetition injuries—Cause for concern. Paper presented at the Australian Physiotherapy Conference, 1983.

Magarian GJ and Nardone DA. Panic attacks and phobias. *The New England Journal of Medicine* 1983, *308*, 342.

Margules DL. Alpha and beta-adrenergic receptors in amygale: Reciprocal inhibitors and facilitators of punished operant behaviour. *European Journal of Pharmacology* 1971, *16*, 21–26.

Markoff RA, Ryan P, and Young T. Endorphins and mood changes in long-distance running. *Medicine and Science in Sports and Exercise* 1982, *14*, 11–15

Mason JW. Organization of the multiple endocrine responses to avoidance in the monkey. *Psychosomatic Medicine* 1968, *30*, 775–790.

Mehrabian A and Russell JA. Emotional impact of environments. *Perceptual and Motor Skills* 1971, *32*, 403–6.

Molnar B and Evans L. The management of phobias. *Patient Management* 1983, Feb., 79–86.

Montgomery SA and Asberg M. A new depression scale designed to be sensitive to change. *British Journal of Psychiatry* 1979, *134*, 382–389.

Morely JE and Levine AS. Stress-induced eating is mediated through endogenous opiates. *Science* 1980, *209*, 1259–1260.

Morgan WP and Horstman OH. Anxiety reduction following acute physical activity. *Medicine and Science in Sport.* 1976, *8*, 62.

Morgan WP, Roberts JA, Brand FT, and Feenerman AD. Psychological effects of chronic physical activity. *Medicine and Science in Sport.* 1970, *2*, 213-217.

Naatanen R. The inverted U relationship between activation and performance: A critical review. In S Kornblum (ed.). *Attention and Performance.* New York: Academic Press, 1973.

Nesse RM, Cameron OG, Cuirtis GC, McCann DS, and Huber-Smitth MJ. Adrenergic function in patients with panic anxiety. *Archives of General Psychiatry* 1984, *41*, 771-776.

Newman RM and Breckenridge JR. A constant temperature water bath calorimeter for measuring extremity heat loss. *Journal of Applied Physiology* 1968, *25*, 447-449.

Neubig RR. Panic attacks and phobias. *The New England Journal of Medicine.* 1983, *308*, 342.

O'Boyle CA, Harris D, Barry H, and Cullen JH. Differential effect of benzodiazepine sedation in high and low anxious patients in a "real life" stress setting. *Psychopharmacology* 1986, *88*, 226-229.

O'Brien CP, Stunkard AJ, and Ternes JW. Absence of naloxone sensitivity in obese humans. *Psychosomatic Medicine* 1982, *44*, 215-218.

Overall JE, Butcher JN, and Hunter S. The validity of the MMPI-168 for psychiatric screening. *Educational and Psychological Measurement* 1975, *35*, 393-400.

Pentland G. *RAAF Camouflage and Markings 1939-1945. Vol I.* Melbourne: Kookaburra, 1980.

Peretti PO. Color-mood associations in young adults. *Perceptual and Motor Skills* 1974, *39*, 715-718.

Peturrson H, Bhattacharya SK, Gover V, Sandler M, and Lader MH. Urinary monomaine oxidase inhibitor and benzodiazepine withdrawal. *British Journal Psychiatry* 1982, *140*, 7-10.

Pitts FN. The biochemistry of anxiety. *Scientific American* 1969, *220*, 69-75.

Pitts FN and McClure Jn. Lactate metabolism in anxiety neurosis. *New England Journal of Medicine* 1967, *277*, 1329-1336.

Polakoff PL. How the well cope with potential illness. *Occupational Health and Safety* 1983, March, 48-52.

Posner MI, Snyder CRR, and Davidson BJ. Attention and the detection of signals. *Journal of Experimental Psychology* 1980, *109*, 160-174.

Rachman S. Fear and courage: Some military aspects. *Journal of the Royal Army Medical Corps* 1982, *126*, 100-104.

Rahe RH and Genender E. Adaptation to and recovery from captivity. *Military Medicine* 1983, *148*, 577-585.

Rahe RH, Conway TL, Vichers RR, Ryman DH, Hervig LK, and Ward HW. Navy company commanders: Serum uric acid and cholesterol variability with job stressors. *Revue Intenationale* 1982, March, 273-282.

Ramm E, Marks IM, Yuksel S, and Stern RS. Anxiety management training for anxiety states: Positive compared with negative self-statements. *British Journal of Psychiatry* 1981, *140*, 367-373.

Ransford CP. A role for amines in the antidepressant effect of exercise: A review. *Medicine and Science in Sports and Exercise* 1982, *14*, 1-10.

Reid P, and Khan SM. Referrals to clinical psychologists: Do results match expectations? *The Practitioner* 1983, *227*, 99-100.

Reisenzein R. The Schachter theory of emotion: Two decades later. *Psychological Bulletin* 1983, *94*, 239-264.

Reynolds HL. The effects of augmented levels of stress on reaction time in the peripheral visual field. *The Research Quarterly* 1976, *47*, 768-775.

Rifkin A, Klein DF, Dillon D, and Levitt M. Blockade by imiprimine or desipramine of panic induced by sodium lactate. *American Journal of Psychiatry* 1981, *138*, 676-677.

Robertshaw D. Hyperhydrosis and the sympatho-adrenal system. *Medical Hypotheses* 1979, *5*, 317-22.

Rose RM. Endocrine responses to stressful events. *Psychiatric Clinics of North America* 1980, *3*, 251-275.

Russell JA. Affective space is bipolar. *Journal of Personality and Social Psychology* 1979, *37*, 345-356.

Russell JA. A circumplex model of affect. *Journal of Personality and Social Psychology* 1980, *39*, 1161-1178.

Sanders AF. Towards a model of stress and human performance. *Acta Psychologica*, 1983, *53*, 61-97.

Savin JA. Excessive sweating of the palms and armpits. *British Medical Journal* 1983, *286*, 580-581.

Schachter S and Singer JE. Cognitive, social and physiological determinants of emotional state. *Psychological Review* 1962, *69*, 378-399.

Schmidtke H. Vigilance. In E Simonson and PC Weiser (eds). *Psychological Aspects and Physiological Correlates of Work and Fatigue.* Springfield, Ill: CC Thomas, 1976, 220-252.

Shacham S. A shortened version of the Profile of Mood States. *Journal of Personality Assessment* 1983, *47*, 305-306.

Sharit J and Salvendy G. Occupational stress: Review and reappraisal. *Human Factors* 1982, *24*, 129-162.

Shaw JA. Comments upon the individual psychology of combat exhaustion. *Military Medicine* 1983, *148*, 223-231.

Sheehan DV. Panic attacks and phobias. *The New England Journal of Medicine* 1982, *307*, 156-158.

Sherman RA. Home use of tape recorded relaxation exercises as an initial treatment for stress related disorders. *Military Medicine* 1982, *47*, 1062-1066.

Shiffrin RM and Schneider W. Controlled and automatic human information processing I and II. *Psychological Review* 1977, *84*, 1-67; 127-190.

Shoenthalar SJ. The value of nutrition in the control and treatment of incarcerated juvenile offenders. *International Journal for Biosocial Research* 1983, *4*, 25-39.

Simon J. The paradoxical effect of effort. *British Journal of Medical Psychology* 1967, *40*, 375-379.

Simonov PV, Frolov MV, Evtushenko VF, and Sviridov EP. Effect of emotional stress on recognition of visual patterns. *Aviation, Space and Environmental Medicine* 1977, *48*, 856-858.

Smart GW, Taunton JE, and Clement DB. Achilles tendon disorders in runners—a review. *Medicine and Science in Sports and Exercise* 1980, 12, 231-243.

Smith RP. Boredom: A review. *Human Factors* 1981, *23*, 329-340.

Snaith RP, Bridge GWK, and Hamilton M. The Leeds Scales for the self-assessment of anxiety and despression. *British Journal of Psychiatry* 1967, *132*, 164-171.

Spielberger CD, Gorsuch Rl, and Lushene RE. *STAI Manual for State-Trait Anxiety Inventory.* San Diego: Consulting Psychologists Press, 1970.

Stave AM. The influence of low frequency vibration on pilot performance (as measured in a fixed base simulator). *Ergonomics* 1979, *22*, 823-235.

Stein L and Belluzzi JD. Brain endorphin and the sense of well being: A psychobiological hypotheses. *Advances in Biochemical Psychopharmacology.* 1978, *18*, 299-311.

Steinmetz JI, Kaplan RM, and Miller GL. Stress management: An assessment questionnaire for evaluating interventions and comparing groups. *Journal of Occupational Medicine* 1982, *24*, 923-931.

Steptoe A, Melville D, and Ross A. Behavioural response demands, cardiovascular reactivity, and essential hypertension. *Psychosomatic Medicine* 1984, *46*, 33-48.

Sullivan HS. *The Interpersonal Theory of Psychiatry.* New York: W W Norton and Company, 1953.

Svebak S and Grassman P. The experience of psychosomatic symptoms in the hyperventilation provocation test and in non-hyperventilation tasks. *Scandinavian Journal of Psychology* 1985, *26*, 327-335.

Tache J and Selye H. On stress and coping mechanisms. in CD Spielberger and IC Sarason (eds). *Stress and Anxiety. Vol. 5.* New York: Wiley, 1978.

Taylor G. Age differences in peripheral letter perception. *Journal of Experimental Psychology* 1982, *8*, 106-112.

Taylor JA. A personality scale of manifest anxiety. *Journal of Abnormal and Social Psychology* 1953, *48*, 285-290.

Teichner WH. A preliminary theory of the effects of task and environmental factors on human performance. *Human Factors* 1971, *13*, 295–344.

Thackray RI and Touchstone RM. *Effects of Noise Exposure on Performance of a Simulated Radar Task.* Report nos FAA-AM-79-24: AD-A-081-065. Federal Aviation Administration; Office of Aviation Medicine, 1979.

Thayer RE. Measurement of activation through self-report. *Psychological Reports* 1967, *20*, 663–678.

Thomas C and Murphy E. Further studies on cholesterol levels in the Johns Hopkins Medical students: The effects of stress at examinations. *Journal of Chronic Disease* 1958, *8*, 661–668.

Treisman AM and Gelade G. A feature-integrated theory of attention. *Cognitive Psychology* 1980, *12*, 97–136.

Trites R and Tryphonas H. Food intolerance and hyperactvity *Topics in Early Childhood Special Education* 1983, *3*, 49–54.

Ursin H, Baade E, and Levine S. (eds). *Psychobiology of Stress: A Study of Coping Men.* London: Academic Press, 1978.

Van Dis H. Hyperventilation syndrome in phobic patients. Paper presented at the 11th European Conference of Psychosomatic Research, 1976.

Van Sell M, Brief AP, and Schuler RS. Role conflict and role ambiguity: Integration of the literature and directions for future research. *Human Relations* 1981, *34*, 43–71.

Vaughan WS. Distraction effect of cold water on performance of higher order tasks. *Undersea Biomedical Research* 1977, *4*, 103–116.

Vaernes R, Ursin H, Darragh A, and Lambe R. Endocrine response patterns and psychological correlates. *Journal of Psychosomatic Research* 1982, *26*, 123–131.

Waksman SA. Diet and children's behaviour disorders: A review of the research. *Clinical Psychology Review* 1983, *3*, 201–213.

Walen SR, DiGiuseppe R, and Wessler RL. *A Practitioner's Guide to Rational Emotive Therapy.* New York: Oxford University Press, 1980.

Warden N, Duncan M, and Sommars E. Nutritional changes heighten children's achievement: A 5-year study. *International Journal for Biosocial Research* 1982, *3*, 72–74.

Westlake M. On course for disaster. *Far Eastern Economic Review* 1983, *122 (141)*, 29–34.

Williams HL, Lubin A, and Goodnow J. Impaired performance with acute sleep loss. *Psychological Monographs* 1959, *73*, (whole no. 484).

Wilkinson R. Interaction of noise with knowledge of results and sleep deprivation. *Journal of Experimental Psychology* 1963, *66*, 332–337.

Winslow CAE, Herrington LP, and Gagge AP. Physiological reactions of the human body to varying environmental temperatures. *American Journal of Physiology* 1973, *120 (1)*, 1–22.

Wright BD and Stone MH. *Best Test Design.* Chicago: Mesa Press, 1979.

Wyndham CH and Wilson-Dickson WG. Physiological response of hands and feet to cold in relation to body temperature. *Journal of Applied Physiology* 1951, *4*, 199–207

Yerkes RM and Dodson JD. The relation of strength of stimulus to rapidity of habit formation. *Journal of Comparative Neurology* 1908, 459–482.

Zigmond AS and Snaith RP. The hospital anxiety and depression scale. *Acta Psychiatrica Scandinavica* 1983, *67*, 361–370.

INDEX

7 8 9 0 1 2 3 4 5 6
A B C D E F G H I J